Inside the Mind of
SCOTT PETERSON

Inside the Mind of
SCOTT PETERSON

KEITH ABLOW, M.D.

Contributing Forensic Psychiatrist on Court TV

Foreword by Catherine Crier

St. Martin's Press ⚏ New York

For these three, who have taught thousands:

Leston Havens, M.D.,
Jonathan Schindelheim, M.D.,
and Edward Shapiro, M.D.

Acknowledgments

I am indebted to Oprah Winfrey for first inviting me to share my views on Scott Peterson with the public. I have profound respect for her daily, breathtaking commitment to disclose the truth about her own life and to heal others by helping them to do the same.

Anne Bird, Scott Peterson's half sister, who appeared with me on *The Oprah Winfrey Show*, also has my sincere thanks. Her insights—some of which were conveyed in her book, *Blood Brother: 33 Reasons My Brother Scott Peterson Is Guilty*, others of which were conveyed to me personally—were invaluable as I researched Scott's story and came to understand the workings of his mind.

Catherine Crier, host of *Catherine Crier Live* on Court TV and author of the number-one *New York Times* bestseller *A Deadly Game*, not only provided the Foreword to this book, but selflessly shared her sources and her rare insights.

Cole Thompson, chief of story development for *Catherine Crier Live*, also provided valuable support.

Gloria Allred, Amber Frey's attorney and a consummate professional, spoke eloquently and openly about her client and about Scott.

I also am indebted to many members of the Latham, Peterson, and Rocha families, who shared their thoughts and feelings about Scott with me. They include John Latham, James Patrick Latham, Jennifer Peterson, Lee Peterson (briefly), and Sharon Rocha. They also include several family members who wished not to be identified by name, but did wish to help me understand the family dynamics they felt had created a killer.

Scott's ex-girlfriend Lauren Putnat offered real insights into Scott's thought patterns and sexual behaviors.

Many others lent guidance, facts, and perspective to this project. They include Brad Garrett of the FBI, Attorney Anthony Traini, Attorney Irwin Zalkin, Dr. Rock Positano, and Sharon Hagan of the Modesto, California, police.

My researcher, Marilyn Firth, spent countless hours scouring the Web and speaking with sources directly to provide me with needed data to build my psychological profile of Scott Peterson.

Larry E. Stauffer Sr. combed the San Diego area, interviewing dozens of people who had known Scott in the past.

Private investigators (who will remain nameless) in three states helped me to hone my vision of Scott.

My agent, Beth Vesel, and my editor at St. Martin's Press, Charles Spicer, treated my work with the same extraordinary focus and energy as they always do. They treated it as their own.

John Murphy, Joe Rinaldi, and Michael Homler at St. Martin's also brought themselves to the project completely.

And Heidi Krupp, of Krupp Communications, accepted the challenge of letting the public know that they could now journey *Inside the Mind of Scott Peterson*.

Simply put, I had the best team any author could possibly have. Even into the early-morning hours, I never felt I was working alone.

Foreword

When I began to write about the murders of Laci and Conner Peterson, I believed that the Modesto police had arrested the right person. Although quiet and charming at first glance, Scott Peterson exhibited what I deemed unusual, if not inappropriate, behavior from the moment his wife went missing.

His relative nonchalance in the early hours of the investigation was puzzling. He seemed emotionally distant from the tragic events and distraught family members as the case unfolded. He was unwilling or unable to make public pleas for Laci's safe return. One month into the investigation the nation learned of his girlfriend, Amber Frey, and watched as Scott finally took to the airwaves to dismiss any connection with his wife's disappearance. He was so bold as to assert that Laci knew of his infidelities and had no problem with such conduct.

Many defenders, including Scott's own parents, claimed that everyone grieves differently. Assumptions about guilt arising from his conduct were unfair. Nevertheless, I believed that legitimate questions were raised by his behavior.

After all, if there is no commonality in human emotions, if we cannot draw certain conclusions from overt behavior, then why read the great writers who seek to illuminate the human condition? Why should we acknowledge the study of psychiatry or psychology?

There is much to be learned from these sources, and never is it more fascinating than when applied to aberrant behavior. Fyodor Dostoyevsky wrote *Crime and Punishment* in 1866. It remains one of the most riveting examinations of a murderous mind in world literature. Yet even the perpetrator, Rodya Raskolnikov, sought redemption at the hands of his inquisitor.

Scott Peterson demonstrated no authentic grief and thus far has sought no such redemption. His behavior seems outside the bounds of comprehension. How does a young man, with no seeming provocation (although it certainly existed in his own mind), commit the premeditated killing of his wife and unborn child? How could he then entertain his girlfriend with fanciful adventures or head to the golf course while those around him were enveloped in grief? Is there a scientific or psychiatric explanation for such a mind and soul?

These are questions that Dr. Keith Ablow has shouldered in an attempt to answer the most difficult question in this case. No longer do most people ask, "Did Scott Peterson murder Laci?" Instead they want to know why.

Like any good investigator, Dr. Ablow began his search at the beginning. Was there something about Scott's family history, his infancy and upbringing, that might provide clues to the tragic outcome on December 24, 2002? Were there early warning signs that might have signaled the need for counseling or intervention? Could anyone have recognized the mask of civility that Scott had donned to cope with the demands of a world he could not relate to? Are there ways of identifying others with the sociopathic tendencies Scott displayed? How can we ever know if such people might turn violent?

Dr. Ablow was able to answer these questions for me as the case unfolded. Now he has authored a compelling examination into the mind of one of the nation's most notorious murderers of the twenty-first century. No stranger to forensic psychiatry, Keith Ablow has testified time and again in such criminal trials. In 1990, his profession became dramatically personal when his close friend, a psychiatric resident, was murdered. Keith responded with a true-crime book, *Without Mercy,* that provided an insider's look at the case and the insanity defense used at trial.

He has put his vast knowledge to use as a novelist in his thrillers featuring psychiatrist Dr. Frank Clevenger. Fortunately, he still finds time to join me on my program, *Catherine Crier Live,* to consult on major crimes and trials around the country.

—Catherine Crier

INTRODUCTION

After all the coverage on Court TV, thousands of articles and several books about Scott Peterson, it struck me that we knew who had killed his wife, Laci, and his unborn son, Conner, but not *why*. Scott Peterson had been found guilty of murder, but he had remained silent during the trial, never taking the witness stand. Peterson's parents and other relatives had testified that his childhood had been very nearly perfect, that it was beyond comprehension that he would dispose of his wife and unborn child in the San Francisco Bay.

But I knew it could not be beyond comprehension. My professional life has been spent in search of the answer to one question: *why?* As a forensic psychiatrist, I have not only treated extremely violent people but have testified in many murder trials about exactly what happens in the minds of men and women who kill. I have told juries precisely how murderers are created, what they feel inside, and what they think in their private moments. In doing so, I have become convinced that there are no unsolvable mysteries of human behavior, even behavior that results in the destruction of others. Every case makes some sort of terrible sense.

This book is an extended version of what I would have told the jury as an expert witness had I been called to testify in the Scott Peterson murder trial. It gives you, the reader, a rare chance to sit in the jury box and hear how Peterson's life story, from infancy, put him on a collision course with the double homicide of Laci and Conner.

At the end of my testimony, Mark Geragos, Scott Peterson's attorney, would have asked me whether I believed his client was insane.

My answer, with medical certainty, would have been yes.

Chapter 1
A PSYCHOLOGICAL "PERFECT STORM"

Before reading this book, you may have believed that the story of the murders of Laci Peterson and her unborn son, Conner, began on Christmas Eve, 2002. That was, after all, the evening Scott Peterson asserted that he had returned home to find Laci's Land Rover in the driveway of their Modesto, California, home, and the couple's golden retriever, McKenzie, in the backyard, alone, with his leash on. At 5:17 P.M. he telephoned his mother-in-law, Sharon Rocha, and told her, "Laci is missing."

If not that fateful Christmas Eve, you might believe the story began a month earlier, on November 20, 2002. That was the night Scott Peterson first met Amber Frey, the pretty, blond, single mother who worked as a massage therapist. The couple shared a drink at the Elephant Bar in Fresno, then dinner at an intimate Japanese restaurant, then a bottle of gin, then had sex in Peterson's room at the Radisson Hotel. Within two weeks Peterson was picking up Frey's daughter, Ayiana, at school and cooking dinner for what looked like an instant family—one he may have preferred to Laci and Conner.

Or you might open the curtain on the murder mystery earlier still. Paying homage to the theory that the pressures of impending fatherhood began to unravel Peterson's psyche, you might begin the day Laci Peterson conceived Conner, about seven months before her husband killed her, weighted down her body, and dumped it in the San Francisco Bay.

There are those, in fact, who see the roots of Scott Peterson's vicious act reaching back years to his discomfort with marriage itself, evidenced by repeated acts of infidelity, including a 1998 affair with Janet Ilse, who once walked in on Peterson and his wife in bed.

Others assert that Peterson was evil incarnate, that the story of the murders of Laci and Conner should begin with Peterson's birth at San Diego's Sharp Hospital on October 24, 1972.

I have a different story to tell. Having researched Scott Peterson and his family of origin by hiring investigators, interviewing relatives, friends, schoolmates, and lovers, placing newspaper advertisements on the West Coast seeking anyone with knowledge of his childhood, posting a Web site dedicated to learning of early traumas in his life, and reading and watching everything I could find in print or on tape about him, I am convinced that Laci and Conner lost their lives to a psychological "perfect storm" that began gathering over the Peterson family over five decades ago and reached hurricane strength in the psyche of Scott Peterson.

The road to the 2002 murders of a young woman full of life and the innocent child she carried truly began on December 20, 1945.

In addition to many sources who wished to remain anonymous, including first-degree relatives of Scott Peterson, I have interviewed his father, Lee, his uncles John Latham and James Patrick Latham, his sister-in-law Jennifer Peterson, his half brother Mark Peterson, and his former lover Lauren Putnat. Anne Bird, Scott's half sister (and author of *Blood Brother: 33 Reasons My Brother Scott Peterson Is Guilty*) shared invaluable insights into him and other members of the Peterson family. Catherine Crier, in addition to providing the Foreword to this book, generously made available several of the sources for her number-one *New York Times* bestseller *A Deadly Game*. Amber Frey's attorney, Gloria Allred, graciously provided me her perspective. And even Sharon Hagan, a profiler for the Modesto Police Department who worked on the Peterson investigation, freely gave me her insights.

After I began outlining the beginnings of my theory about Scott as a guest on *The Oprah Winfrey Show*, I received hundreds of e-mails from viewers who said it helped them understand the truth about him for the first time. It made it possible for them to actually see into his soul. Anne Bird and Laci's mother, Sharon, agreed. And other members of Scott Peterson's family have since.

I am a forensic psychiatrist. My work has included evaluating dozens of murderers, rapists, pedophiles, and other violent criminals and testifying about them in district, state, and federal courts. Without exception, my task has been to find the story that explains not *what* happened to victims but *why* it happened— *why* some people destroy others. In order to do so, I have had to journey deep into the psyches of men and women without empathy, capable of brutal acts. And I have become a relentless burrower for the truth about such people. My mind does not rest until I find it. Because once I do, I have my reward: I realize again that nothing and no one is beyond human understanding—not even those we call monsters.

It has been no different with Scott Peterson. I have spent countless hours on this journey into his mind, sleepless nights when I forced my thoughts in the direction his must have gone the day he took the lives of his wife and unborn child. I have forced myself to feel what he might have felt as he drove home after leaving them in the Bay.

I am certain that I know. Now you will, too.

Chapter 2
DEATH

On December 13, 2004, a jury in Redwood City, California, having found Scott Peterson guilty of the murders of Laci Peterson and the couple's unborn son, Conner, unanimously sentenced him to death. They had deliberated his fate for eight hours and twenty-three minutes over the course of three days.

Peterson himself sat emotionless as he received his death sentence. His mother, Jackie, and father, Lee, remained silent.

Prosecutors had painstakingly made their case. Nearly two years earlier, on Christmas Eve, Peterson had killed his pregnant wife, wrapped her body in a tarp, loaded it into his truck, and used the ruse of going fishing to dump it into the San Francisco Bay, weighted down with cement anchors he had made himself.

According to the testimony of Modesto Police Detective Al Brocchini, Peterson had foreshadowed the plot back in 1995. He had told a friend named Miguel Espidia that if he wanted to get away with killing someone he would dispose of the body by tying a bag around its head, fastening weights to its hands, and throwing it into the sea. Fish would then eat away at the flesh so that identification of the victim would be impossible.

Laci's remains had no head, no hands, and no feet. Conner's body was also badly decomposed. They were identified through DNA testing.

Scott Peterson had not only killed his wife but discarded his own child. He had remained eerily stoic while Conner's condition at autopsy was described in court.

Prosecutors had painted the portrait of a remorseless killer. They had proved Scott was a pathological liar who had first told Amber Frey he was unmarried, then tearfully confessed he had "lost" his wife, that he wanted to make a new life with Amber and her twenty-month-old daughter. He had continued the romance by phone after killing Laci, calling again and again with fabricated stories about traveling around Europe when he was actually at home in Modesto, playacting another role: the concerned husband spearheading the search for his missing pregnant wife.

About two years earlier, on New Year's Eve day, he had called

Amber, pretending to be in Paris, near the Eiffel Tower, watching fireworks with friends named Jeff, François, and Pasqual. "The New Year's celebration is unreal. The crowd is huge . . ." he told her.

Unreal, indeed.

"The crowd's huge?" Amber asked.

There was static on the line. "Amber, if you are there, I can't hear you right now, but I'll call you . . ."

Peterson hung up, then phoned her back. A dog was barking in the background. It was actually McKenzie, his golden retriever, an unwelcome intrusion on the fantastic tale he was spinning. "There is this fucking dog next to this hotel," he said.

"This what?" Amber asked.

"This dog that just keeps barking."

"Really?"

"I want to kill it," Peterson said.

Amber asked him whether he had made any New Year's resolutions. "Oh, I'm sure there's all kinds of things that I want to do better about myself, but I've got nothing," he told her. "I can't think of anything."

Amber Frey was not the first woman for whom Scott Peterson had fashioned an alternate identity. There had been Janet Ilse, the woman who learned Peterson was married only after walking in on him in bed with Laci when he lived in San Luis Obispo. There was Katy Hansen, a California Polytechnic coed whom Peterson also dated back then, and who was also convinced he was single.

According to Hansen, Scott first denied ever being married or engaged, then retracted that version of his life story in favor of being divorced.

Hansen assumed Scott was an only child, since he never mentioned his half brothers John, Mark, or Joseph, or half sister Susan. She met his roommates, but not a single one of his friends.

It wasn't until graduation day that Hansen, fully expecting her relationship with Scott to continue, abruptly came face-to-face with reality when Scott's wife, Laci, walked up to him, gave him a lei of flowers, and kissed him on the cheek in a way that left no doubt that he belonged to her.

According to Shawn Sibley, who introduced Amber Frey to Scott, Scott claimed that he had pretended to be a vegan to ingratiate himself with another woman during college, strictly avoiding the consumption of any animal products for the six months they dated. The minute she flew home from school, he went out for a hamburger.

Peterson's deceptions were not limited to women. He lied to classmates about having received a golf scholarship to Arizona State University. He ordered phony diplomas online, including a Bachelor of Arts in religious studies from Arizona State and two degrees from the University of San Diego.

Scott Peterson seemed to believe he had the ability to slip the binding of his life story and insert new, fictional chapters at will, to re-create himself à la Jay Gatsby, obliterating the past and rewriting the future again and again and again.

When he was arrested April 18, 2003, after the bodies of Laci and Conner washed up onshore—another annoying reality intruding into his fabricated existence—it seemed as if he were prepared to do it again. He had used his mother's name, Jacqueline, on California Department of Motor Vehicles forms he needed to buy a used Mercedes Benz for $3,600 cash. He had removed his wedding ring. He had dyed his hair, eyebrows, and his new beard orangey blond. His car contained $14,932 in cash, an undisclosed amount of Mexican currency, four credit cards (including one in the name of his half sister Anne Bird and another in the name of his mother), his half brother John's driver's license, camping equipment, a fishing rod and reel, an entire wardrobe including twelve pairs of shoes and a cowboy hat, four cell phones, sleeping pills, and twelve tablets of the male sexual performance–enhancing drug Viagra.

Peterson offered no resistance and showed no panic when police pulled him over and handcuffed him, nor when they later placed him in leg irons and waist chains. He made one of the three calls he was allowed from jail to friends of his, Heather and Mark Richardson, to let them know he had made them some cookies, but wouldn't be able to send them.

One of the arresting officers noted that Peterson's demeanor was "calm, devoid of grief, concern, or anger," and that, most of the time, he "displayed a distant stare toward the wall across from where he sat and occasionally smiled while talking. . . ."

A little more than an hour after being told that DNA testing had confirmed that the remains found in the Bay were those of

Laci and Conner, Peterson downed a double cheeseburger, fries, and a vanilla shake.

Perhaps the officers wondered how killing could come so easily to him. Perhaps they wondered why Scott Peterson seemed unmoved by his own plight. How could he be thinking of the mundane when he was shackled, under arrest for the murder of his wife and unborn son?

I know that jurors, Laci's family, and Scott's parents wondered the same thing as he sat, unmoved, when he had been found guilty and, later, when he was sentenced to death.

Scott's half sister Anne Bird noticed how he seemed unfazed even by his impending transfer from the Maguire Correctional Facility in Redwood City to life imprisonment at San Quentin. As she documented in her book *Blood Brother: 33 Reasons My Brother Scott Peterson Is Guilty*, he told her, "Once this goes to appeal, it'll be all right. . . . I mean, this has been just ridiculous. This entire thing has been a big waste of time. I mean, I know it'll take a while. These appeals can drag on. But San Quentin won't be so bad. It's pretty famous. It's an old, historical building, overlooking San Francisco. It'll be a wait, but you get more privileges in the long-term facilities."

He was mostly upset that only paperback books would be allowed at San Quentin. "I like hardbacks," he told Anne. "I'm trying to read them as fast as I can because I can't take them with me."

In fact, Scott was already writing chapters of his life story beyond his release from prison. "Yeah," he told Anne, "after the sentencing, they'll take me over to San Quentin. A whole SWAT team will come out, and they'll drive up the interstate at a hundred miles an hour. But I'll get out. When it's over, I'll get out.

"And I won't need much, either. By that time, I'll have been in a six-foot cell for a while, so what would I need? Just a little space. I wouldn't even mind if I had to sleep with a toilet next to my head; I do that now.

"Everything I need, I'll find right at Home Depot. Not much at all. I'm going to live a very simple life. Everything is going to work out fine, sis. Don't worry about a thing."

Don't worry about a thing? How could Scott Peterson not be worried? How could he not break down, screaming or crying or begging for forgiveness?

I will tell you the reason: Scott Peterson had already been spiritually dead a very long time. He had walked among us as an emotional vampire feasting day-to-day on the life force of others, particularly women.

Neither handcuffs nor chains can restrain a man whose soul has no core, no center. His thoughts and feelings can travel anywhere, carried on the black wings of his imagination.

Such a man will not be frightened by the specter of lethal injection. For he has already left us.

You cannot kill a man who is already dead.

Scott Peterson had been emotionally strangled, beginning in infancy. By the time he was a child, he was already well on his way to becoming a psychological cadaver, merely imitating a live person, everything genuine about him already buried under layer upon layer of denial. Having shut down his real feelings in order to short-circuit unbearable pain, he could not resonate with anyone else's pain. His empathy, the ability to relate to the suffering of others, had been extinguished. He was free from the emotions that connect us, one to another—whether grief or fear or hatred or love.

No wonder that Peterson would refer to himself in terms reserved for corpses. On December 2, 2002, beaming at his lover, Amber Frey, and her magical little girl, Ayiana, he told Amber, "Look at me, I've got a rigor-mortis smile."

Rigor mortis, of course, is the stiffening of muscles that occurs after death, as lactic acid builds up in tissues deprived of oxygen.

On another occasion, Peterson reportedly told Amber he had "rigor mortis" in his hands, apparently because they were causing him pain at the time.

And back in high school, whether as a Freudian slip, an intentional pun, or even a typo, the theme of death seeped into the official good-bye he submitted for publication in his high school yearbook. It read: "Great things and good deads await all of us."

When Scott Peterson killed his wife, Laci, I can tell you with certainty that he felt almost nothing. At most, there may have been a twinge of anger or sadness, some distant echo of what he might have felt as a boy, during his own gradual demise. I can picture him shaking his head at the feeling, confused by it, like the intrusion of other painful realities into his fabricated existence.

I can also tell you Peterson never wept a real tear for the unborn child he destroyed. The entire concept of innocent life, after all, was alien to him.

Lest we forget, he had never cried for himself, despite having barely taken his first breath when his own destruction began.

Chapter 3
DECEMBER 20, 1945

THE GATHERING STORM

Shortly after 9:00 P.M. John H. Latham, a married father of four, and Scott Peterson's maternal grandfather, prepared to leave his office at the salvage yard and tire shop he had recently purchased at 2190 Main Street in downtown San Diego. His cash register had about two hundred dollars in it—receipts for that day—and he usually carried as much as four hundred or five hundred dollars in his wallet.

Latham changed out of his work clothes into street apparel and went outside, probably to do a final check on the yard, filled with hundreds of tire carcasses.

He only got a few steps before someone struck him in the head with a three-foot length of rusty pipe, crushing his skull and leaving him to die in a pool of his own blood.

Frank Flynn, an employee coming to work to turn on the electric tire molds, found Latham's body at 7:00 A.M. the next morning, lying faceup beside the bloody pipe.

Latham's wallet was missing. His cash drawer was empty. A light still burned in his office.

Latham's wife, Helen, was called by police and given the tragic news. According to an article published in *The San Diego Tribune*, she had not reported her husband missing the prior night because she knew that he sometimes "stayed out with the boys."

Deputy Coroner E. A. Turner performed an autopsy and confirmed the cause of death to be "a very vicious blow from a blunt instrument."

A death notice published in the *Tribune* read:

LATHAM—December 21, John Harvey Latham, husband of Helen Latham, father of John Harvey, Jr., Patrick, Jacqueline and Robert John—Johnson Suam Mortuary

Two days before his murder, Latham had fired Robert Sewell, a twenty-eight-year-old handyman. Sewell was initially questioned by police and released. But after boasting about the killing to friends some four years later, he was again detained. He then confessed under intense interrogation.

According to Sewell's confession, he returned home after attacking his former boss with a pipe and told his wife he had "struck it rich." He gave her most of the money he had stolen, and the couple used it to vacation in Los Angeles a few days later.

Sewell was sentenced to life in prison for the murder he committed December 20, 1945. He died in San Quentin, where Scott Peterson now sits on death row, awaiting execution for murders he committed fifty-seven years later, on December 24, 2002.

One more parallel, for those reticent to believe that today's murder mystery can share pages with another almost six decades old. Anne Bird told me that while he was living with her after Laci's disappearance and before being charged with murder, he stored a large metal flashlight in an inconspicuous location in her home. "It looked a lot like a length of metal pipe," she said. "I kept telling him to take it with him when he left here, but he never would. And now it's lost. I just can't help wondering whether that was the murder weapon. I mean, his grandfather was killed with a lead pipe. Is it too crazy to think he was repeating things?"

Chapter 4
WIDOWED

John Latham's wife, Leeta Helen Hixon-Latham, never recovered from her husband's murder. Varying reports cite worsening lung problems, a debilitating skin disease, being brokenhearted, or simply being emotionally ill-equipped to parent four children alone as the reason she gave up her children, bypassing her own sister and placing them in Nazareth House, an orphanage run by Catholic nuns.

One of those children was Jacqueline Helen Latham, Scott Peterson's mother. She was just two years old when her father was killed.

A two-year-old cannot comprehend a murder. No matter how her father's sudden disappearance from her life is explained to her, she will feel abandoned, unloved, and perhaps unlovable. She may wonder whether she has done something terrible to drive her father away, or cause God to take him away. She may wonder whether her mother will be the next to go.

In this case, of course, her worst fears would be realized. She would be taken to a cold, damp facility run by women clad in black and left there.

It is hard to imagine the emotional trauma suffered by a young girl who abruptly learns her father will never come home again, then is sent away by her mother, to be raised by strangers. But it is easy to imagine how such a girl might build walls around her, intuiting that to survive such catastrophic trauma she must stop feeling the waves of despair and rage that feel as though they will shred her developing psyche.

I remember my wife, Debbie, telling me that my own daughter would hold my photograph and cry on the rare occasions that I traveled away from home for more than a few days when she was two or three years old. I can scarcely imagine how Debbie would have broken the news to her had I died on one of those trips. And I can hardly fathom the mental gymnastics my daughter would have had to employ in order to compartmentalize that sudden loss and not be emotionally paralyzed by it forever.

I have a patient who did lose his father when he was three

years old. Now seven, he keeps a photo album full of his father's pictures in his bedroom and still weeps over them unexpectedly, from time to time. It brings his mother to tears, too, which at least gives him the certain knowledge that he is not alone in his pain, that he is loved by someone who also loved his dad. That is a genuine gift, and I hope it sustains him.

In his book *Darkness Visible*, the author William Styron (who authored *Sofie's Choice*, among other great works), whom I met years ago at his home on Martha's Vineyard, wrote of how the death of his mother when he was thirteen sparked a lifelong battle with nearly incapacitating alcoholism and major depression:

> The genetic roots of depression seem now to be beyond controversy. But I'm persuaded that an even more significant factor was the death of my mother when I was thirteen; this disorder and early sorrow—the death or disappearance of a parent, especially a mother, before or during puberty—appears repeatedly in the literature on depression as a trauma sometimes likely to create nearly irreparable emotional havoc. The danger is especially apparent if the young person is affected by what has been termed "incomplete mourning"—has, in effect, been unable to achieve the catharsis of grief, and so carries within himself through later years an insufferable burden of which rage and guilt, and not only dammed-up sorrow, are a part, and become the potential seeds of self-destruction.

After he lost his mother, Styron still had one parent who cared deeply for him. But how does a two-year-old girl not lose all faith in all human beings (including herself) when a man kills her father for several hundred dollars, and her mother then packs her belongings and sends her to an orphanage?

Having worked with children who lose parents and with adults traumatized by such early losses, I know they often have lifelong difficulties maintaining healthy relationships. They become afraid to believe that those they love will stay with them, afraid even to feel love at all. Fearing the loss of anyone they connect with, they develop complex personality strategies to avoid genuine intimacy, to keep others at a distance. And these strategies often are universal, playing out not only in adult romantic relationships and adult friendships but with their own children, with whom they never develop genuine emotional connections.

For Jackie Peterson, there was even more loss around the corner. At Nazareth House, boys were so obsessively separated from girls that Jackie would rarely see her three brothers, John, James Patrick, and Robert.

"We didn't hardly play together," John told me about those years. "We were separated as siblings. My brother Patrick has never gotten away from what happened to him there as a kid."

Jackie's visits with her mother were restricted to one per week.

Adding insult to injury, Jackie fell ill, developing severe asthma. She was dependent on the sisters at Nazareth House to administer her medication.

Quality food wasn't plentiful. According to an article published in the *San Francisco Chronicle,* Jackie recalls eating outdated food and bread that the sisters begged for door-to-door. "We got eggs maybe once a week for a treat," she said.

Near-perfect parenting by custodians might not salvage the emotional well-being of a child who is cleaved from both parents and three brothers, and then finds herself confronting her own medical problems and poverty, but nothing like near-perfect parenting was the rule at Nazareth House, where Jackie Peterson would spend the next ten years.

"It was prison," James Patrick Latham told me. "My younger brother ran away ten times, but it's like in the military—where the hell are you going? They just wait for you at home and bring you back."

It was apparently even tougher for girls at Nazareth House.

"If the girls were pretty the nuns cut their hair and tried to make them ugly," James Patrick said.

One woman raised in another Nazareth House orphanage wrote of the nuns there:

The Nazareth House nuns were very very frightening. Oh, how they hammered down on us kids! It was worse than thunder and lightning . . . They were so brutal. . . .

> When [they] beat me with those big, big sticks, [they] left
> me feeling pretty sick. Two characters is what [they] were
> like. Jecky and Hyde . . .

According to Jackie's brother James Patrick Latham, even
worse happened.

"My brothers and I didn't have sexual abuse," he told me,
"but it did happen to the girls there. And if the girls said anything they would embarrass them in front of all the other girls.

"This one overseer had access to all of them. Some girls are
just starting to say something now. There are lawsuits starting."

Attorney Irwin Zalkin, who represents some of those plain-
tiffs, including some who resided there when Jackie Peterson
did, told me, "Nazareth House was a cesspool of pedophilia. We
represent one woman who was fourteen when she lived there.
There's an adjoining parish, and she would make lunches for the
priests at the rectory. She would be sent with lunch for one
priest who would sexually abuse her nearly every day. When it
became known, she was sent for counseling with a counseling
priest, who also abused her."

"There was also abuse by nuns," Zalkin told me. "Victims
were digitally penetrated."

In addition to sexual abuse, Nazareth House was reportedly
notorious for physical abuse. "We're talking about kids beaten,
locked in closets, physically manhandled, spanked, hit with
sticks, hit with rulers," Zalkin said. "I know of one victim who
was repeatedly beaten and thrown in showers with hot scalding
water."

Despite this rampant abuse, Jackie Peterson has denied feeling any substantial psychological pain while at Nazareth House.
"I felt fortunate that I had a roof over my head, three meals a
day, and was educated," she told the *San Francisco Chronicle*.
"We knew that God loved us, and that just took over everything."

When you wonder at Scott Peterson sitting stoically with his
defense team to receive his death sentence, when you shake your
head at him telling Anne Bird that he will find everything he
needs at Home Depot after his release from San Quentin, think
about Jackie living at Nazareth House, feeling fortunate to be
there.

Chapter 5
ABANDONMENT

Jackie Peterson left Nazareth House at age thirteen to care for her ailing mother, saying good-bye to the nuns who had raised her. It was hardly the first time she had had to sever human connections.

She received a scholarship to attend a Catholic girls' school twenty miles away. Despite having to live with and play nurse to a woman who had given her up to an orphanage, Jackie might have convinced herself she was finally at home, with someone who loved her.

Shortly after Jackie graduated high school, however, her mother died. The obituary read:

Mrs. Helen Latham

Mrs. Helen Latham, 55, of 4584 W. Point Loma Boulevard
died Wednesday in a hospital. Recitation of the Rosary
will be at 5 P.M. Sunday in Berdsley Funeral Home.
Requiem Mass will be at 9 A.M. Monday in Sacred Heart
Catholic Church. Internment will be in Holy
Cross Cemetery.
Here 30 years Mrs. Latham was a native of Oklahoma.
She is survived by three sons, John, Patrick and Robert,
a daughter Jacqueline, all of San Diego, and a sister.

Jackie was eighteen and alone. Again. She had already lived through the murder of her father, separation from her mother and brothers, poverty, the climate of abuse at Nazareth House, the debilitating symptoms of her own asthma and, now, the death of her mother.

Survivors of trauma much less severe than Jackie's often retreat behind walls of pleasantries, denying all pain and suffering, donning rose-colored glasses to avoid seeing the frightening shadows falling upon them. In so doing, they are merely borrowing against the increasing debt to be paid to the truth—the unavoidable grief and understandable rage that must eventually be expressed. Refusing to do so allows those feelings to fester beneath the surface, twisting in on themselves, becoming more and more intense—and more toxic. If not aired by one generation, they will be expressed by the next, or the next. Because, in the end, the truth always wins.

This is why psychiatry is a true healing art, and why I love practicing it. My job is to hold my patients' hands and open the early chapters of their life stories, often ones filled with intense emotions they have avoided, born of crushing disappointments and losses in childhood and young adulthood. When we do so together, they are relieved of the terrible burden it is to hide such feelings, and they can devote the mental energy they once used to suppress the truth to getting on with the most positive aspects of their lives.

I often use the metaphor of an infection to describe why avoiding painful realities ultimately destroys people—why feeling the grief or rage or shame, rather than avoiding intense emotion, is always the best course.

Imagine an infection in your arm. Walled off by the body, it has become an abscess. It hurts—a lot. It hurts even more to touch it. You try to ignore it, but the pain grows too intense. You use painkillers to stop it. They work, but only for a while. Then the area grows redder, warmer, and angrier than ever.

You have a choice to make. The thought of a surgeon exploring the abscess, incising it, opening it up to the air, is frightening. The surgeon could find worse disease. What if the infection has gone to the bone? What if a cancer lurks at the center of all the inflamed tissue? Could life itself be lost by looking deep inside?

If you think that more intense resolve to not think about the infection is the answer, or that stronger painkillers will cure it, you are wrong. The infection will burrow deeper still, and only cause more destruction.

Now imagine that the infection is contagious—that your children can catch it from you.

It will take courage, it will cause you some suffering initially, but there is only one way to truly move forward toward well-being and real strength. It is to grit your teeth and probe as deeply as need be to root out every bit of the infection, every bit of the ugly truth. Because only that journey can truly save you.

Jackie Peterson took a different path. She sought solace in the arms of men. The year her mother died, she became pregnant and delivered a little boy named Don on April 2, 1963.

She had another chance for a real family.

Imagine the desperate hope Jackie must have felt that she had found someone who adored her, who would help her create a real home, help protect her, never turn her away.

It was not to be. Her lover left her—another staggering loss.

Abandoned again, her baby now nothing but a reminder of a broken promise, Jackie gave him up for adoption.

Don was raised by a couple by the name of Chapman, who also adopted a baby girl. He eventually married, settled in Pennsylvania, and had three children.

I vividly remember my wife holding our son just after he was born, tears streaming down her face, telling me she already had the intuition that he would grow to be a great man. She knew she would be bringing him to a safe home, with a father who would love him—and her. But I can force myself to imagine the horrible shock it would have been to learn that I would not be going home with her, that I did not want to be part of any growing family, that the life she had imagined for herself and her growing family was merely a fantasy, that the baby she had birthed would forever be tied to feelings of abandonment and desperation.

Any woman might then wonder, if only she had never become pregnant. Then maybe she would not be alone. Maybe she would still be in the arms of someone who had once promised he would stay with her forever.

Maybe new life would forever be tied in that woman's mind with lost love, with the death of romance.

Maybe, in quiet moments of despair, that woman would think her baby would be better off dead rather than abandoned by its father.

Did Jackie Peterson ever think that before she sent her baby boy away forever?

Did Scott Peterson think that before he sent his baby boy to the bottom of the sea?

But Jackie was still determined to find love somewhere on

the bleak landscape of her existence. During 1964 she became pregnant again, this time by her brother's best friend. On July 8, 1965, she gave birth to a baby girl named Anne (now Anne Bird).

Surely now, Jackie must have fantasized, she had the makings of a family. After all, the father of her baby was tied not only to her but to her brother.

But a dismal reality again cast its shadow over all her hopes. She was again abandoned by her lover, who was already with another woman.

The baby in her arms again represented abandonment. Birth was again the harbinger of a kind of death.

Pregnancy, the potential joy of a growing family, had again proved itself to be a sham, nothing but a symbol of being alone and unloved.

Perhaps all the ugly memories flooded into Jackie's mind. The terrifying news that her father would never come home again. The equally unthinkable news that her mother would no longer be willing or able to raise her. The realization that her brothers would be separated from her at Nazareth House. The first day she could not draw a breath and was diagnosed with asthma. The tears of little girls beside her being beaten or scalded or raped by nuns or priests. The sudden death of her mother.

Or maybe Jackie was already skilled at not thinking any of those thoughts, not feeling her pain, turning away from the festering abscess in her psyche.

She gave her second child up for adoption.

Every day in America, single, financially challenged women who only want the best for their children give them up for adoption. But doing so twice within two years is unusual and testifies to Jackie's ability to not only bury her emotions but to sever attachment to other human beings, even her own offspring.

Jackie went back to finding warmth the only place she ever had, in the arms of men who wanted to have sex with her. During 1966 she gave birth to another son, by a third man. And, yet again, she was abandoned.

According to Anne Bird, who reunited with her mother decades later, Jackie wanted to put this third baby, who she had named John, up for adoption, too. She wanted to get rid of another reminder that she was unloved, maybe unlovable. She was ultimately dissuaded from doing so by her pediatrician, who, according to Bird, "told Jackie she could no longer have child after child and give them away."

Perhaps the good doctor should have done more. Perhaps he should have considered whether Jackie was a proper parent to send a little boy home with. In giving away two children and considering giving away a third, she was extraordinary in her capacity to remain emotionally detached from others.

Jackie raised John as a single mother until she met and married Lee Peterson, who had three children from a prior marriage, had grown up dirt poor, and was working for a trucking company. Lee later adopted John.

Did Jackie miss the fact that Lee Peterson and her mother, Leeta Helen Hixon Latham, had very nearly the same first name? Or did she believe it was a sign that she was being healed, that God was paying what He owed her for taking her father and mother?

Jackie finally had what she had so desperately sought: A man who would stay with her. A new family. But underneath that pretty picture were all the old traumas, all the unspoken rage, all the unspeakable grief.

Jackie bought a little dress shop in La Jolla called The Put On.

How appropriate.

According to a first-degree relative of his, Lee Peterson may have been the perfect coconspirator to help Jackie keep her demons at bay. He had grown up following his mother on her housekeeping jobs. His father had lost all the family's money in a failed business and repaired typewriters for a living. His boyhood home lacked indoor plumbing. And for a time, Lee buried all those memories under the facade of an expensive California home in Rancho Santa Fe, and Ferrari and Rolls-Royce automobiles he struggled to make payments on. According to one source, he used a pseudonym for a time when his finances were in disarray.

"He is very private," his first-degree relative told me. "It's almost to the point that I don't know who he is. I don't think he ever knew that himself. He is not someone comfortable with real emotion—his own, or anyone else's."

"I don't think he liked kids," the source went on. "They're too real. They don't fake anything. I think he left his first wife partly because he couldn't stand having them around."

A year later, Jackie and Lee Peterson had a child of their own. A boy. They named him Scott. And despite Scott contracting pneumonia shortly after birth and needing to be placed in a plastic oxygen chamber, despite the fact that it was not clear whether he would even survive, Lee's memory of him was as a happy, "shiny" baby.

Chapter 6
THE FIRST WEEKS OF "LIFE"

Scott Peterson was born by cesarean section on October 24, 1972. While Lee Peterson gushes about Scott's full head of hair and distinctive looks and beams when describing Scott's siblings' excitement as they gazed through a plate-glass window at their new, "shiny" baby brother, there were less happy moments.

Shortly after birth, Scott contracted pneumonia and needed to be separated from his mother. He was placed in a plastic chamber that delivered oxygen and controlled humidity and air pressure. His life was at risk.

It is noteworthy that never during their testimony at trial did Jackie or Lee Peterson talk in depth about any fear that they might lose their infant son, or any distressing memories of him with fevers or struggling for air, or the pain of learning that they would have to turn him over to doctors to be placed in a plastic chamber, away from them.

Maybe they felt none of that.

Whether Jackie and Lee would be able to empathize with it or not, however, Scott's early and sudden separation from his mother had the capacity to permanently damage him psychologically.

According to the famed late psychiatrist John Bowlby, infants suffer real trauma when removed from their mothers shortly after birth. They experience crashing waves of emotion, including periods of protest (experienced as intense anxiety), despair (experienced as grief and mourning), and then detachment and denial (as a defense against their feelings). And these waves of distress and helplessness can set the stage for lifelong difficulties attaching to others in meaningful, loving ways.

Researchers even believe that the roots of a sociopath's twisted personality—including inability to appreciate the suffering of others, preoccupation with fantasy, and inability to plan for the future—can sometimes be traced to early, sudden separation between an infant and his or her mother.

When life begins with a panic much like drowning, unable to bring enough air into your lungs, followed by isolation under a plastic dome, with the cold reality of masked nurses and doctors peering at you, their eyes filled with worry that you will die, your body pierced unpredictably and uncontrollably by needles, it should come as no surprise that you may wish to "disappear" psychologically from the earth, to crawl back inside a womb built hastily inside your own mind, defending against pain, denying all reality.

As Bowlby writes in his landmark work,

> States of anxiety and depression that occur during adult years, and also psychopathic [sociopathic] conditions, can . . . be linked in a systematic way to the states of anxiety, despair, and detachment . . . that are so readily engendered whenever a young child is separated for long [even for a few weeks as an infant] from his mother figure. . . . Whereas during later life it is often extremely difficult to trace how a person's disturbed emotional state is related to his experiences, whether they be those of his current life or his past, during the early years of childhood the relationship between emotional state and current or recent experience is often crystal clear. In these troubled states of childhood, it is held, can be discerned the prototype of many a pathological condition of later years.

Many newborns, especially those born prematurely, need to spend time apart from their mothers shortly after birth. They don't grow up to be killers.

Still, can we dismiss the connection between Scott Peterson being cleaved from his mother and him feeling nothing about cleaving his own son Conner from Laci? Can we ignore the terrible symmetry between an infant who is unable to breathe due to an infection filling his lungs and an almost full-term fetus unable to breathe because his oxygen is being cut off while his mother drowns?

Can we fail to draw a four-generation bloodline connecting the murder of John Latham for about six hundred dollars, the beginnings of the spiritual death of two-year-old Jackie Peterson when her mother sent her away to Nazareth House, the emotional suffocation of Scott Peterson, and then the stillbirth, underwater, of baby Conner?

In Scott's case, of course, no one need make the argument that his pneumonia and resulting isolation in a plastic chamber fully explains him dying spiritually and then only pretending to be alive and connected to other living beings.

Imagine who you might be today if you could truthfully begin your autobiography (as Scott Peterson could) this way:

> I was born to a mother whose father had been murdered. At age two she was sent away by her mother and grew up in an orphanage that has been called "notorious," a "prison," and a "cesspool of pedophilia." She put her first two children up for adoption, considered putting her third child up for adoption, and then had me. I was quickly taken from her and spent my first days in a plastic oxygen chamber, struggling for air. She then brought me home to live with a man whose close relative has claimed he had no emotional insight into himself or anyone else and disliked having children around during his prior marriage. I knew from day one that if I caused these people any trouble whatsoever, I was as good as gone. I was afraid to think anything or feel anything, let alone say anything remotely negative. Hell, I was afraid to breathe. In a very real way, I was forced to suffocate myself to death. Dad would tell you I was a shiny, good little boy. He wasn't one to notice that I already had a rigor-mortis smile.

The chances of Scott Peterson ever being encouraged to have real emotions, let alone vent them, was close to zero.

His separation from his mother—and, ultimately, from himself—was not to be just for the weeks following his birth. It was a life sentence.

John Bowlby knew there were different kinds of separation. "Yet a further difficulty," he wrote,

> turns on the fact that a mother can be physically present but "emotionally" absent. What this means, of course, is

that, although present in body, a mother may be unresponsive to her child's desire for mothering. Such unresponsiveness can be due to many conditions—depression, rejection, preoccupation with other matters—but, whatever its cause, so far as her child is concerned she is no better than half-present. Then again a mother can use threats to abandon a child as a means of disciplining him, a tactic that probably has an immeasurably greater pathogenic effect than is yet recognized.

Chapter 7
HOME "LIFE"

Scott Peterson must have learned early on that being anything but the perfect child would not be tolerated by his parents. I believe he was in a perpetual state of unconscious panic that his mother (who had given away two other children and who had considered giving away her third) would abandon him and that his father would do nothing to save him.

To Jackie Peterson, after all, children symbolized her own abandonment by the men she had hungered to keep in her life. After suddenly losing her father, three lovers had deserted her when she gave birth. And her husband, Lee, the only man who had ever stayed with her, had reportedly left his prior marriage partly because he wasn't comfortable living with his children.

Jennifer Peterson, Lee's former daughter-in-law and the mother of four of his grandchildren, including five-year-old twins, a three-year-old, and an eight-year-old, told me, "It was very strange. Lee just never seemed to form any attachment to any of my children."

Despite her husband's apparent difficulty warming up to children, and her own history of giving a baby girl and boy up for adoption, Jackie Peterson called her new family "the Brady Bunch."

She couldn't risk Lee being "uncomfortable" with his home life. It had to be perfect. He might leave her alone with her children, just as he had his last wife. Her sons, Scott and John, would have to be nearly invisible to avoid bothering him and putting her at risk of being abandoned yet again.

There are myriad and subtle ways a mother can tell her son that he must cease to exist as a person, that his true self must essentially disappear.

When she fails to respond to his instinctual needs, insisting that he eat, for example, when he is not hungry, and neglecting to feed him when he is, he learns that his appetite is irrelevant.

When she demands that he eat foods he dislikes, he learns that his tastes are beside the point. He will swallow what he is fed, period. He will pretend not to mind. And, once he turns himself completely inside out psychologically, he will actually enjoy it.

When she forces him to nap when he would prefer to play or read, he learns his internal clock is broken, and that he must look to others to know when he is tired.

When she lets him cry himself to sleep rather than comforting him, he learns that his loneliness and protests and sadness and tears are to no avail—ignored, useless, as though not even real. And he will soon stop feeling those feelings and be silent at bedtime, already an expert at putting his desperation and anger to sleep.

When she stops talking to him for hours or days when he disappoints her, he cannot miss the terrifying symbol that she has the capacity to cut him out of her life, and to effectively end his. And he will strive—swear a blood oath, if necessary—to never let her down.

If he ever shows her how angry he is becoming, she might tell him he has no right to feel that way and should "leave her house" if he isn't happy with the way she runs it. And, terrified at being cast out to fend for himself, he will disguise his curling lip or swallow his harsh words or learn to ignore the clenching of his jaw, and bury his rage deep inside him.

When he laughs at something, she can shake her head quizzically, as though there is nothing funny at all, and he will learn not to trust his sense of humor, to resist smiling or laughing at things that amuse him. He will instead check the faces of others to know precisely when they are beginning to smile, so he can mimic their expressions, and laugh when they laugh. "We have exactly the same sense of humor," he will tell them. And they will believe they are with a blood brother.

When she tells him enough times that he "makes no sense," he will start to believe her and will be loath to express any opinions, instead soliciting the ideas of others, and restating them as his own. "We think alike," he will tell them. And they will believe they have found a kindred spirit.

He will slowly kill himself off, and become a person imitating a person, a hunter-gatherer of the "emotions" and facial expressions and ideas that will receive the best reception, that will get him some of what he needs from a world he has learned is unfeeling and unpredictable and cruel and potentially lethal.

He will start down the road to sociopathy.

And there are so many more ways a mother could push a child there, from his earliest years.

She could force him to use the toilet when he is resistant to doing so, then ridicule or punish him when he fails to harness his bodily functions perfectly to her will.

She could simply fail to show any joy at signs of his developing personhood—his favorite color, favorite song, favorite animal, favorite food or piece of clothing or storybook. "Green?" she could ask, with a shrug. "You like *green*? I always thought it was such a boring color." And from that day forward, he will hate the color green. He will ask his roommates or friends or girlfriends the colors they like and profess to like the very same ones. How coincidental. How lucky to find such a perfect friend, or a lover so much like you.

She could disagree with him about reality—the color of a shirt, whether a promise was ever made to go somewhere after school, when a period of punishment was slated to end.

As Anne Bird has noticed about her mother, Jackie, "It is very, very easy for her to make up stories, dates, insist things happened that never did. I would show up somewhere to meet her and she would say. 'No, I told you it's tomorrow.' My brother Don says the same thing about her. She tries to change facts to suit her."

Anne also noticed that Jackie told several different versions of her own life story, changing the dates important events had taken place, even altering her age when her father was murdered.

Another source close to the family told me, "Jackie lies about anything and everything. She would not confirm your recollection or view of anything, if it didn't suit her."

Another way a mother can alter reality and drain the life force from her child is to objectify him. Jackie Peterson called Scott Golden Boy, a clear sign that she expected him to be perfect for her, with no rough edges. Shiny.

A child's response to parents who respond so negatively to his individuality and humanity will be to withdraw, to playact at being perfect, to hide his own instincts and fears and desires and dreams and likes and dislikes behind fortresslike walls. In order to gain their "love," avoid rejection, and stay safe from their potential rage, he will literally kill himself emotionally.

Scott was so quiet as a baby and toddler that Lee and Jackie once forgot about him while they dined in a restaurant and walked out without him.

Anne Bird once observed, "I think Jackie treated Scott like a dress-up doll from day one, someone who could have the best manners of anyone, ever. Even when he was an adult, she would always smile at him, and you could just see her thinking, 'He's the perfect person.' But there was something scary about him—like a puppet, not real."

Indeed, during his first year of life, Jackie carried Scott around so much that it became a family joke that his feet never touched the ground.

She quickly convinced him he was extraordinary, but that he was also wholly owned and operated—by her. Without her adoring eyes, her ceaseless compliments, her reminders to him that he was the perfect person, he would be no one and have nothing. He would be worthless.

"If this could happen to any family," a source close to Lee and Jackie Peterson told me, "it doesn't surprise me one bit that it happened to this one—because of the disconnectedness from reality. Jackie says everything with a smile, but it's a predatory smile—like, 'If you cross me, you're going down.'

"My opinion is that Jackie isn't all there. I feel like she may have had a . . . not a mental illness, but . . . she seemed very . . . You never get a straight answer from her. It's crazy making. You could get different answers to the very same question at different times. And if you ever brought that up, or made any other wrong move, you knew you were going to fall out of her good graces. Then you would be nothing to her, dead in her world."

Lee Peterson, Scott's father, told me how quickly his son learned to behave (or to give up all autonomy), to lose all the rough edges of personality and behavior that real people have, to be perfect. "We never had to swat him or anything. Ever. We just told him what to do and he did it. He just wanted to please. He was never in a fight, never said a bad word in front of us about anyone. He never had a single run-in with authority."

Joann Farmer, a friend of Jackie Peterson's during Scott's boyhood, told an investigator of mine that Scott was "painfully shy" growing up.

"He [Scott] was a little bit reticent, stoic maybe," Joan Pernicano, another friend of Jackie's, said in an interview published in the *San Francisco Chronicle*. "My son bounced off the walls, but Scott wasn't that way. He was quiet and polite. He's a smiler, and when he smiles, his whole face lights up."

He already had the perfect smile. He had learned that facial expression very well. He had it down, pat.

In fifth grade, Pernicano recalled, teachers at Painted Rock Elementary School in Poway, California, picked the perfectly well-behaved youngster to work as a school crossing guard. "He was very serious about his responsibility," she said. She laughed, remembering how a driver had become frustrated with Scott when he kept younger students from crossing the street when another car was still a block away.

And Pernicano described Scott for television talk show host Bill O'Reilly as, "very nice, very kind, very genteel." He was, she said, "respectful" and "very close to his family."

"This is the last person in the world you could see doing anything like this [murdering his wife and unborn son]," Lee Peterson told me.

That is, of course, unless you were to look beneath the shiny, golden surface, the facade of perfection, behind what the late psychiatrist Hervey Cleckley has called the "mask of sanity." Because people do not abide their destruction with equanimity. They become slowly, quietly, increasingly paranoid, secretive, and very, very angry.

Psychologist Arno Gruen, in his book *The Betrayal of the Self,* recalls one of his patients who put it this way, "You cannot touch me if I am as you wish." He goes on to describe the young man as extraordinarily good at intuiting "the thoughts and wishes of other people."

"By accommodating himself to their wishes," Gruen writes, "he protected himself from the perils of openness or commitment. He simply performed what others expected of him, he himself was not involved in the actions. . . . His autonomy existed only in his own imagination."

Infected with suppressed rage that had been building for generations, convinced that he had to play dead to live with his parents, Scott Peterson's soul was already under siege.

Three decades after John Harvey Latham was killed without a struggle in his salvage yard, his grandson was quietly dying at home.

Chapter 8
LIKE FATHER, LIKE SON

One of the things a child losing himself, dying psychologically, is likely to do is to imitate one of the people close to him, particularly one of those "caring" for him. When anything original to that child, anything that comes from his or her true, core self, is met with disdain, mirroring a caretaker can feel like the only safe way to go.

If your life must be an act, beginning as an understudy makes perfect sense.

A child who thinks he may be discarded, essentially left alone to die, will cling to anyone he can, even the person threatening to kill him. And that child will deny that the person he is embracing and cherishing is the one out to get him.

It is simply too frightening, unthinkable, for a young mind to admit that a person charged with caring for him is also the one destroying him.

Children of alcoholics who beat them are often the clingiest children of all, staying as close to their violent parents as possible, often staying in the house where they were abused long after they could be out on their own.

This phenomenon is a distant cousin of the well-known Stockholm syndrome, in which hostages come to embrace their kidnappers. Cozying up to those with the power to destroy you is a natural response to being at their mercy.

It is no surprise that Lee Peterson encouraged this father-son mirroring. He believed his son should do the same things he enjoyed doing. Why should he cater to the boy's own tastes, after all? It would be much easier for Lee to pretend they did not exist. He and his son could spend a lot more time together that way.

Lee liked to golf, so, when Scott was about five years old, he started teaching Scott to golf. And, no surprise, Scott seemed to like it.

The Petersons enrolled Scott in Junior Golf during grade school. His first tournament was at Presidio Hills in Old Town, San Diego. And although he got badly beaten, he showed no disappointment. In fact, he said he loved the experience.

How many little boys who perform poorly in a sport in front of a bunch of other little boys react stoically? How many say they loved being beaten? How many parents would consider that absence of emotion normal, even desirable?

When Scott was fourteen, Lee Peterson promised to buy him a Ferrari if he shot par at the country club where Scott worked part-time. "Imitate me," he might as well have said, "ignore who you are, and I will give you the world."

Maybe the Ferrari was supposed to be just like the one Lee drove, the one he could scarcely afford. But when Scott actually did shoot par at age sixteen, there was no Ferrari as a prize. This one wasn't just a financial illusion, it was entirely imaginary.

Lee liked to fish and hunt, so he taught his son how to do those things, too. And, no surprise at all, Scott seemed to like them just fine.

Lee had left trucking to run a shipping and packing business called San Diego Crating, so he took his young son to work with him. He said it gave him "confidence" to have Scott with him. And, no surprise at all, Scott seemed to like hanging out on the job with Lee, too.

Scott never complained. Not once. He never got bored, never cried to go home, never said he'd rather hang out with a friend, never refused to go.

He liked to call his dad Chief.

One of Scott's nicknames was Trooper. His middle name was Lee.

"He was like Mr. Perfect [as a youngster]," Lee Peterson told the *San Francisco Chronicle* after Scott was arrested for murder.

Mr. Perfect. Of course, he was. What else could he be?

"Scott and Lee were really like best friends from day one," a source close to the family told me. "There was no boundary there. It wasn't healthy."

And the truth is, Scott and Lee Peterson may have had more in common than either even imagined.

"Lee had a really, really bad temper," a family member of his told me. "He and Jackie were all nicey-nice on the surface, but you just knew not to cross them."

Beneath the surface, Lee's emotions were churning—and, his family member believed, potentially dangerous.

"Jackie told me," the family member said, "that she and Lee had to get separate beds because he attacked her a few times in his sleep. He was sleeping and started hitting her and tried to strangle her. It happened more than once."

"I believe he has been on psychiatric medication to try to keep his moods stable for many years, and keep his anger under control," the source added.

Another first-degree relative of Lee Peterson confirmed that he has taken psychiatric medication for a decade or more. "Lee has very violent dreams," the relative said. "I don't know if the medicine is for that or for something else."

What dreams might Scott Peterson have had as a child?

He might have had a recurring nightmare that both his parents had died, sleep being the only venue in which his mind could embrace his unconscious yearning to be free of them, free to start being a real person.

He might have dreamed that he was lost, unable to find his way somewhere he very much needed to go. After all, he was journeying further and further from his inner self every day. And finding the way back was looking more and more unlikely.

He might have dreamed he was a little girl, that even his gender, like every other part of his truth, was in doubt.

He might have conjured the image of parasites inside his brain, eating away at his very thoughts, interfering even with the clarity of the nightmare he was having at that very moment.

He might have awakened to a wet or soiled bed, having been psychologically blocked from achieving full control over any part of his existence, including the workings of his own body.

Or maybe he had a nightmare that someone was chasing him, intent on doing him in. Perhaps, exhausted from running, sweat beading up on his forehead, losing ground, he would begin to turn to look at his pursuers, only to wake, screaming, before he could see their faces. And maybe the moonlight filtering into his room would be enough to illuminate the smiles of his mother, Jackie, and father, Lee, telling him to go back to sleep, that everything would be all right, that he was just having a bad dream, again, that he was as safe as safe could be, the best boy in the world, in a perfect family, with parents who absolutely loved him to death.

Chapter 9
MR. PERFECT

Scott Peterson perfected his mask of sanity as he made his way through grade school, Rancho Santa Fe Junior High School and the University of San Diego High School. Dead inside, a person imitating a person, he was gathering more mannerisms, turns of phrase, and honing the charming sense of humor that would hide how empty he felt, how much rage at being psychologically murdered was smoldering at his core.

He was becoming a true psychopath—now known in psychiatric literature as a sociopath—divorced from his own emotional reality and that of others, left to guess at how people felt about themselves and the world around them.

He was voted the "friendliest" student in eighth grade. He was polite and respectful to everyone.

He had seen, after all, what would become of him were he to drop his mask and disappoint his parents. According to Anne Bird, Scott's brother John, six years older than Scott, had gotten into trouble as a teenager and had been in an accident in Lee's truck. Jackie and Lee already considered him a problem child and immediately sent him away to live with relatives out of state.

Jackie had not given John away as a baby, she had waited until he was a teenager. She never gave a guarantee of unconditional love.

"John wanted to come home so much," Anne Bird told me, "but they just left him there, even though he talked about how desperate he felt. They just considered him a bad kid. They always had. They wrote him off."

Mark Peterson, Lee's son from his prior marriage, had learned the same harsh lesson about his father. The two worked for a time together in Lee's San Diego Crating business. But when they disagreed about the business, Lee summarily fired him. "He didn't just fire him, though," Jennifer Peterson, Mark's ex-wife told me. "He said very hurtful things to him. It was really as if he was talking to a complete stranger, firing some stranger he'd never met who'd been on the payroll a couple months or something."

Scott was not about to let any such thing happen to him. He

would never rebel, never disappoint. He would always be the good son, even if it killed him.

Maybe things would have turned out differently if Scott's paternal grandfather had lived longer. Lee Peterson's father had always been kind to his grandson. But within hours of his moving in to live with Lee and Jackie and their children in Rancho Sante Fe during 1986, he was dead. Jackie and Lee had taken him out to dinner and he had then died in his sleep.

I am unaware of any comprehensive police investigation into that death.

Scott was popular with some students in his high school, while remaining all but invisible to others. He was already very good at choosing those who would respond well to him acting out the part of a person, and those he had better steer clear of.

Ed Ventura, who played on the golf team with Scott, told the San Diego *Union Tribune,* "We always wanted him to play, but when it came to wanting to be around him we would stay away. He was a loner. At school he was the kind of guy you would walk by and not even notice. He was a good golfer, that's all."

A very good golfer. He played his freshman year alongside Phil Mickelson, who became a top PGA player. And when Mickelson graduated in 1998, Scott became the team's leader. He earned most valuable player honors two out of four years and was named to the *San Diego Tribune*'s All-Academic team three out of the four.

Scott's high school golf coach, Dave Thoennes, has described him as "dependable" and "well-disciplined."

But, according to Thoennes, he was even more controlled than that. Thoennes told the *San Francisco Chronicle,* "He was very respectful. I don't think I ever heard Scott use foul language. Some kids will hit a bad shot and go into all kinds of antics. Scott would hit a bad shot and go to the next one. I don't think I ever saw him get out of control."

"Especially in high school, a lot of guys would lose it on the golf course," Scott's former teammate Brian Tasto, now a San Diego dentist, has said. "I always thought Scott was real even-tempered."

Never an obscenity. Never out of control. No emotion. Not real.

A mask of sanity. According to Hervey Cleckley's research into sociopaths:

> All the outward features of the mask are intact; it cannot be displaced or penetrated by questions. . . . The examiner never hits upon the chaos sometimes found on searching beneath the outer surface of a paranoid schizophrenic. . . . Only very slowly and by a complex estimation or judgment based on multitudinous and small impressions does the conviction come upon us that, despite these intact rational processes, these normal emotional affirmations, and their consistent application in all directions, we are dealing here not with a complete man at all but with something that suggests a subtly constructed reflex machine which can mimic the human personality perfectly. This smoothly operating psychic apparatus reproduces consistently not only specimens of good human reasoning but also appropriate simulations of normal human emotion. . . . So perfect is this reproduction of a whole and normal man that no one who examines him in a clinical setting can point out in scientific or objective terms why, or how, he is not real.

Scott earned good grades. He even tutored the homeless. Who could find any fault with him? Certainly not his mother or father. And wasn't that the idea?

Apparently, though, reality was wearing thin for Scott. The facts didn't provide the perfect image he craved, the kind he had learned he needed in order to gain "love" from others (or at least to avoid being abandoned by them). Instead of just obsessively controlling his story, he began to take liberties with it. He wanted to glitter like gold for everyone, not just Jackie and Lee. He gave his high school golf teammates the impression that he had won a golf scholarship to Arizona State University, where Phil Mickelson had helped the school win the NCAA gold championship that year.

Doug Tammaro, Arizona State's associate sports information director, however, told the *San Francisco Chronicle* that Scott Peterson was "never on a roster." Tammaro could find no evidence that Scott ever played for the school at all.

And Lee Peterson has admitted that Scott had only talked informally to the golf coach at Arizona State, who encouraged him to try making the team as a "walk-on."

But that wasn't a story Scott could live with. "It was probably a mistake sending him there," Lee Peterson said, "because it was such a big golf school."

Translation: It was probably a mistake sending him there, because the coaches there didn't agree that Scott was extraordinary. They weren't up for writing more fiction into his life story. They didn't keep pace with the false worship heaped upon him by Jackie and Lee, in order to own his soul.

The truth would never be enough for Scott Peterson, because it would always be rooted in the fear of abandonment and the pain of being dehumanized.

He went to back to work on his mask of sanity.

Scott had begun trying to impress women, wining and dining them, lying to them to keep their affection.

There are very few things that could remind a man like Scott Peterson that he was alive at all, present on the planet, not a ghost. Sexual excitement was one of them, a stark symbol that he was at least anchored inside his body, that he could feel something, that he could at least connect—if only at a physical level—with someone. He needed that. And he would need it more and more as the last remnants of his real soul, his emotional truth, his humanity, receded further and further from his grasp.

According to Catherine Crier's book *A Deadly Game*, Scott had two girlfriends in high school. One was Stephanie Smith, a tenth-grader who dated Scott when he was a senior. Scott reportedly romanced her with gifts, flowers, and jewelry, including a special ring on Valentine's Day.

But Stephanie had dated Scott about four months when she heard rumors that he was seen holding hands with a classmate of theirs named Dawn Hood. Dawn had been seen driving Scott's car.

"When Stephanie confronted him about the rumors, however," Crier writes, "she found his response hard to believe. Dawn and he had swapped cars, he told her, so she could try out his new wheels. When pressed, Scott vehemently denied there was anything going on with Dawn. The two were 'just friends.'"

When Stephanie asked about the hand holding, Scott told her he held hands with lots of his friends.

Stephanie broke up with him and returned the gifts he had given her.

Perhaps Scott was puzzled. Why didn't Stephanie believe him? Maybe it was because he hadn't seemed angry with her for doubting him. He could try that next time. Or maybe he should seem hurt, maybe even cry.

Hervey Cleckley explained why a sociopath may believe he can lie convincingly, even when caught red-handed. Cut off from real emotion, he assumes others lack emotional intuition, that others will believe what he tells them, not what they *sense* and *feel* and *know in their hearts*.

Cleckley wrote:

> However intelligent, he apparently assumes that other persons are moved by and experience only the ghostly facsimiles of emotion or pseudoemotion known to him. However quick and rational a person may be and however subtle and articulate his teacher, he cannot be taught awareness of significance which he fails to feel. He can learn to use the ordinary words and, if he is very clever, even extraordinarily vivid and eloquent words which signify these matters to other people. He will also learn to reproduce appropriately all the pantomime of feeling, but . . . the feeling itself does not come to pass.

During the investigation into Laci Peterson's murder, Dawn Hood confirmed that she and Scott had indeed dated, for about eight months, until he went off to college. He had not only romanced her but had managed to win affection from her parents, with whom he sometimes spent time even when Dawn wasn't around.

No doubt Scott was easy to "adopt" into the Hood family. He was an expert at figuring out how to make his own parents want to keep him around. He probably never said an unkind word to them. He probably never swore. He complimented their daughter and them ceaselessly. He was, no doubt, a pleasure to have around.

They didn't know him at all.

Another passage from Cleckley:

The surface of the psychopath [synonymous with sociopath] . . . shows up equal to or better than normal and gives no hint at all of a disorder within. Nothing about him suggests oddness, inadequacy, or moral frailty. His mask is that of robust mental health.

Who was the Scott Peterson who graduated from the University of San Diego High School? Who was the young man who lied about being recruited to play golf at Arizona State, who lied to keep the affection of two teenage girls at the same time, and who bade farewell to his classmates promising, "Great things and good deads await all of us?"

Scott Peterson was a sociopath imitating a complete human being, a psychological cadaver desperately embellishing his own death mask. His demise had begun the day he was born. He had never known any real love in the world. He had been sold a bill of goods by his mother and father that he was extremely special and worthy of adoration. He had only that thin myth to cushion him from the reality that they had never loved *him* at all, had never really cared to know who *he* even was, had kept him in constant terror of being discarded, convincing him utterly that clinging to life with them required burying *himself*. And he had buried that self so deeply that he had lost track of where to find it. He would forever recognize and be drawn only to these clues:

- The goal of winning the adoration of women who did not really know him would always be a powerful force in his life, an echo of the false love of his mother.

- Conquering women sexually would be both physical evidence of his existence (through his sexual excitement), a substitute for real emotional warmth, and a kind of revenge for his own spiritual murder.

- The rage of others would intrigue him, hinting at the cauldron boiling in the epicenter of his own psyche.

- The appearance of being a financial success would be an important distraction, as it had been to his father, from the ordinariness of his talents.

Last, but by no means least, the idea of birth would forever conjure deep inside him very, very powerful, hidden associations with death—especially his own.

Chapter 10
THE "REAL" WORLD

There was some rough going for Scott Peterson when he left home for Arizona State University. There was no golf scholarship waiting for him. He didn't play for the team at all.

Peterson has said that he disliked the golf coach.

Maybe the coach didn't praise Scott enough. Maybe he hadn't been briefed by Jackie or Lee about how extraordinary their Golden Boy was. Or maybe they did tell him, and he just didn't buy it.

In any case, Arizona State is a big school. It is easy to be lost in the crowd. For Scott Peterson, already teetering on the brink of nonexistence, dependent on the very conditional "love" of his parents, it would have been intolerable.

He lasted just one semester.

Homesick, he returned to live with Jackie and Lee in the Morro Bay cottage they had envisioned as their retirement home.

The spiritual annihilation of a child by his parents is like a noose that gets tighter and tighter, sometimes for decades. And, in the worst cases, the parents never let go of the rope. The child journeys into the world, already struggling for air, and learns that no one "loves" him like his mother and father, who lied to him about his worth, inflated it into a myth impossible to "live" up to. He feels out of place, depressed, and angry. And so he returns to them, to play the role they scripted for him, the one that never had anything to do with who he really was inside, the one destined to end with his complete annihilation.

Scott started going to work with Lee at San Diego Crating and playing golf with him, just the way he had as a little boy. The Golden Boy. He was Lee's understudy again.

Maybe that's the whole story about Scott's first semester of college, maybe it isn't. You just never know with the Petersons.

According to Scott's half sister, Anne Bird, Scott left behind something other than an injured ego in Arizona. "The way I heard it," she told me, "he got a girl pregnant there. Jackie flew out, and the girl got an abortion. I guess you could say she's the ideal person to call [in a situation like that]."

Within six months of moving away from home, Scott had almost created new life, but had then acquiesced to it being extinguished, reportedly with the help of his mother.

The calculus seemed to repeat itself again and again in the Peterson family: birth equals death.

Maybe if Scott's lover had decided to keep her child, maybe if Scott had been surprised by an instinct in him to nurture that baby, maybe if genuine feelings of love *from* that human being had crept up on him and and deep into him, reminding him that he was indeed a real person, worthy of real warmth and affection, he might not have become a murderer. Maybe he would have been won over by life, brought back from the dead.

It wasn't to be.

That really matters. Every event in a person's life story really matters. I treated one violent man, for example, who told me that remembering a single sentence spoken to him by a single teacher in the fifth grade had, more than once, kept him from murdering someone. He kept hearing it at critical moments. The teacher had said: "I don't care what everyone else thinks, I know deep down you're a good person. You don't really want to hurt anyone."

He had carried those words like a shield against his great potential to destroy others.

I know you're a good person. Six words spoken by one kind soul to another soul. My patient never forgot them.

If I practice until my hundredth year, I will never lose my sense of wonder and amazement at the potential we have as human beings to heal one another—or hurt one another.

As stressful as it would have been for him, if Scott Peterson could have held his own child when he was a college freshman or sophomore, if he could have looked into an infant son or daughter's eyes and seen something innocent inside himself, there is a chance that the flame of life barely flickering deep inside him would have begun to burn more brightly.

Perhaps if his girlfriend had put it this way, "I would never destroy this baby, Scott, because it is a part of you, and I love you," then we might never have watched Laci Peterson's body pulled from the San Francisco Bay, or Scott Peterson on trial for her murder and that of his unborn son.

We have the capacity to heal one another.

We also have the capacity to destroy one another.

According to Anne Bird, the page of Scott's life story that was written the first time he impregnated a woman was coauthored by his mother. And her stories had always tended away from the truth and toward darkness: Birth equals death.

Chapter 11
"LOVE LIFE"

After leaving Arizona State University, Scott Peterson attended Cuesta Junior College in San Luis Obispo. He played golf for two years. But he didn't even dominate that small school's team. According to Pete Schuler, Cuesta's sports information director, quoted in the *San Francisco Chronicle*, Peterson "just missed qualifying for the state meet his sophomore year."

Again according to the *San Francisco Chronicle*, Peterson moved out of Jackie and Lee's house, telling them, "I've had the greatest parents. You don't owe me anything."

Translation: We aren't going to talk about you stealing my life. Ever.

In 1994, he transferred colleges again, to California Polytechnic State University, also in San Luis Obispo. He began taking courses toward a bachelor of science in agriculture.

Scott's original plan had been to concentrate in international business. When he changed focus, he told his father, "I guess instead of driving a beamer [BMW] and drinking martinis, I'll be driving a pickup and drinking beers."

To Scott, he was just trading one acting job for another. The props would be changing, but his life was nothing more than a scripted drama, anyhow. What did it matter if he was traveling the world engaged in high-level negotiations between corporations or traveling to farms, selling fertilizer (which was eventually the way he would earn his living)?

As in high school, Scott kept his mask of sanity firmly in place. His professors at Cal Poly remember him as respectful and serious.

Jim Ahern, who taught agribusiness, told the *Chronicle*, "He seemed more mature than most. He was pleasant to deal with. I wouldn't mind having a class full of Scott Petersons."

No doubt. In a class of robots or puppets, there would be no horsing around, no difficult questions, no one looking bored, no one challenging authority, no one angry over the scoring of an exam. Everyone would "love" the subject material and compliment the teacher on his remarkable ability to make it come "alive." Everybody would seem perfectly content—on the surface.

Scott ended up only taking two courses each quarter at Cal Poly, maybe to earn the money to go to school, maybe because he was finding performing at that school just as challenging as he had at Arizona State and Cuesta Junior College.

He waited tables at a restaurant called the Pacific Café. While working there, he met an eighteen-year-old waitress named Lauren Putnat and started dating her. He romanced her with flowers and gifts, like his high school girlfriends. He let her drive his Porsche.

"You could tell his mother had raised him right," Putnat told me. "He was the ultimate gentleman, regal in a way. He was very, very mature and very polite. I never even heard him swear."

"They are very close," Lauren said of Scott and his mother. "He was a mama's boy. She literally worried if he would cut himself or scratch himself. She babied him."

When mothers "baby" their sons in the way Lauren was describing it is another way of loving them *to death*. They are depriving them of learning to take care of themselves, suggesting to them again and again that some terrible end will come to them if they are not in constant contact with home, that the world is a dangerous, unpredictable place where even a nick or a scratch could be a calamity. Better to keep oneself safely under wraps, even if it feels like suffocating.

Scott and Lauren dated for about eighteen months, and Scott started to talk about marriage. It was probably what he guessed she wanted to hear. But Lauren wasn't ready for that kind of commitment. And there was something about Scott that had started to wear thin with Lauren. Something robotic. He expressed very little emotion. "He was very bland," she said. "He didn't laugh or cry like a normal person would."

He wasn't spontaneous, either. "Everything had to be planned. It was right out of a movie. It was always Scott's vision of what a woman would desire. He didn't just go on dates, he executed dates: I'm talking about picnics with strawberries and wine and this and that. Yummy cookies with raspberries. Everything was perfect. He strove to be the best man he could be, but it was a little boring after a while. It didn't feel real."

What Lauren couldn't quite put her finger on was the fact that she wasn't dating a real person. She was dating a person imitating a person. He was romancing her in the way he thought a man should, maybe literally the way he had seen it done in movies. Gifts, flowers, picnics with wine, hanging on her every word, smiling when she smiled, laughing when she laughed, never getting angry, never admitting to having a bad day, never dropping his mask.

"I think he got the whole formal thing from his parents," Lauren said. "They used to have teatime at home. I mean, *teatime*, like, in their garden, as if they were at Buckingham Palace."

There had always been something strange about sex with Scott, too. He seemed to like it, but he never came forward with any particular desires or needs of his own. "He was sexual and willing to try new things," Lauren told me, "but he didn't instigate much at all. I would try anything, and he was open to it, but he wanted to do whatever I wanted to do. He would conform to my desires and just follow along. It was kind of boring."

Being with a dead man usually is. In bed, like everywhere else, Scott Peterson was absent, buried inside himself, very unsure of everything about himself, including his manhood, trying to do the things he guessed would give a woman pleasure.

He was undoubtedly very attentive and very patient, studying his lover for the beginnings of her excitement, learning what made her close her eyes, begin to arch her back, cry out with pleasure. But his studied way of making love would always be from some distance. He could penetrate women, but would never let them penetrate his soul. He would be incapable of meeting his lover in ecstasy, focused only on delivering her there, using his anatomy not to bring her closer but to drive her deeper into her own arousal, further away from him. Even his expressions of pleasure would be fake, mirroring hers.

"He would moan like a girl," Lauren told me. "I would laugh sometimes because it was kind of funny. He would be the type to lay down and say, 'Okay, bring it on.' More like a woman. He was very submissive."

It must be said that Scott's behavior in bed would make perfect psychological sense if he had been sexually abused as a boy, especially by a woman. Sex might then always trigger the willingness in him to submit. And, as the most powerful event in his young life, he might seek to repeat it, again and again and again, recruiting woman after woman to subtly playact his domination.

His sexual fantasies, were he ever to have shared them, probably would have included actual domination, being restrained by a woman, told what to do, punished if he did anything displeasing to her, rewarded if he listened closely to everything she was saying, performed exactly as she expected, intuited exactly what she needed.

He would have been most excited by scenarios in which his own enjoyment, desires, and even his own orgasm were irrelevant—where he was taken.

When and where, we cannot avoid asking, did Scott first learn to "moan like a girl"? Who first taught him?

I do not have a definitive answer, but while writing this book, I kept coming back to the question. And as a psychiatrist, I have learned that there must be a reason for that.

As Lauren slowly withdrew her affection, Scott became increasingly overbearing and jealous. Unable to see her as a person, he would have been unable to accept that she could have her own *feelings* about him, unable to fathom that she might not *love* him, might not *desire* him, might not be *happy* spending time with him.

As a mere facsimile of a person, with his emotional wiring shorted out, gone dead, Scott would not be able to fully grasp that Lauren was a real human being, that she had the right to make her own decisions, to follow her *heart*.

Ultimately, she broke off the relationship.

Smart girl.

A man like Scott Peterson would have a hard time believing that any woman could choose to leave him. He was, after all, the Golden Boy who had grown into the perfect man. But the rejection would cut him particularly deeply because his life story was one of being completely and utterly rejected as a human being by the first woman he had ever known—his mother. How could it be that he had submerged his entire personhood under decades of denial, had traded in his humanity for a seductive mask of sanity, and that it still wasn't good enough? It was his worst fear come true, that his acting wouldn't be good enough for the audience he really cared about—a woman who had said she loved him, and was now abandoning him.

In Scott's mind, every woman would forever be Jackie: a person he believed he needed to trick in order to get what he needed in the way of affection, a person who might abandon him at any time, a person who might secretly be plotting to destroy him.

Scott tearfully begged Lauren to reconsider. And even after she had made it plain that there was no chance for them, he would show up uninvited at her home, trying to win her back. "He was very afraid and panicked about losing me," she said.

Chapter 12
LACI

A few weeks after Scott and Lauren broke up, Scott began dating Laci Rocha, a fellow student at the California Polytechnic State University who was majoring in ornamental horticulture— the use of plants and flowers to beautify the grounds around homes and buildings.

Laci was a pretty, petite, and bubbly brunette who had been a high school cheerleader. She had a sunflower tattooed on her left ankle.

While Scott told his family that he was immediately smitten with Laci, Lauren Putnat remembers things differently.

"He was still trying to get me back after he met her," Lauren told me. "He was still trying to come back to me and date me for a long time. He would come over and cry and be very upset."

Scott also used Laci to try to make Lauren jealous.

"He would bring Laci into the section of the Pacific Café where I waitressed, trying to get me interested in him again," Lauren told me. "She would cry and have to be pulled out of the rest room. She knew from very early on that he was a ladies' man."

Maybe. But Laci had a way of focusing on the prettiest part of any picture, fixing things up until they looked pristine, at least on the surface. She had chosen to spend her professional life decorating with flowers. She loved watching Martha Stewart, the grande dame of domestic elegance, perfection, and tranquility (who, we all know, wasn't the perfect person she pretended to be, either).

As Anne Bird writes in her book *Blood Brother*, Laci was "determined to make the world a prettier, more appealing place."

"With Laci, it wasn't about being snobby," Bird continues. "It was about doing things properly. She loved detail. She would have made Martha Stewart proud, imposing order and beauty on everything she touched."

Laci even had the capacity to smile through physical pain. During her pregnancy, she had traveled to Disneyland with Bird and other members of the family, including Scott. She was suffering a lot of pain in her lower back.

Bird writes, "Laci looked over at me and smiled that big,

dimply smile of hers. 'My back's killing me,' she said. That was Laci: Even when she was complaining about her aching back, she was smiling to beat the band."

Laci's resolve to overcome or ignore darkness and focus on pretty things, in fact, may be one reason she had attracted a violent man before ever meeting Scott Peterson. For a time, she lived with her high school sweetheart William "Kent" Gain. Gain was physically abusive toward her during their relationship. He later attempted to murder another girlfriend of his and is serving a fifteen-year prison sentence in the state of Washington.

Scott Peterson's way of courting a woman would be a lock-and-key fit with Laci's idealized vision of romance. The flowers, the picnics, the perfect cookies he liked to bake, teatime with his parents in their garden.

No doubt, Laci wanted to believe someone could be that perfect, a ready-to-serve husband who would make Martha Stewart proud.

She didn't notice that he looked perfect because he was embalmed, a vampire, the living dead, seducing her in order to feast on her aliveness, her energy, her blood.

For Scott, Laci's willingness *not* to look at the dark side would have reassured him that he would never be forced to confront his suffering, would never be seen as anything but a Golden Boy, never truly be seen at all.

Laci would never peer behind his mask of sanity or hold up a mirror and make him look at himself.

Scott quickly introduced Laci to his family with the stilted cliché: "I hope this is the future Mrs. Peterson."

The couple were engaged just before Christmas 1994 and moved in together just before Christmas 1995. They spent a great deal of time with Scott's parents, and Laci planted flower gardens for Scott's mother, Jackie.

Laci was the second woman Scott had lived with, his mother having been the first. Maybe he hoped for better than being suffocated to death this time. Maybe he hoped for resurrection.

Or maybe the timing just felt "right" to him. Just before Christmas 1945, of course, Scott's grandfather had been killed, setting in motion a series of events over the course of nearly six decades that had effectively destroyed him.

Being so close to the anniversary of her father's murder, after all, Christmas must have always been a forced celebration in Jackie Peterson's house as Scott grew up. The themes of birth and rebirth must always have mingled with those of loss and grief and death.

As the author Robert Pirsig has written, "What sort of future is coming up from behind I don't really know. But the past, spread out ahead, dominates everything in sight."

You can't outdistance the past. In the end, the truth—especially any truth we turn our backs on—always wins.

Seven years after moving in with Laci, just before Christmas 2002, Scott would destroy her and his unborn child, finally shattering the myth that he had been born into the perfect family, a Golden Boy, when, in truth, he was closer to stillborn.

Think about it: Christmas 1945; Christmas 1994; Christmas 1995; Christmas 2002. The dates line up like the cylinders on a combination lock.

You can't outdistance the past.

Chapter 13
PAST BECOMES PRESENT

It was around the time Scott met Laci that he learned he had two siblings he'd never met. Jackie had never told him about Anne Bird or Don Chapman, the two children she had given up for adoption, even though Don had actually found her and met with her a year before.

Anne Bird, who appeared with me on *The Oprah Winfrey Show*, is a constant observer of people and an open and honest person. Her book, *Blood Brother: 33 Reasons My Brother Scott Peterson Is Guilty*, her comments on *Oprah*, and her subsequent discussions were very important in helping me confirm the level of denial and lack of feeling in the Peterson family.

"Scott and Jackie seem very similar to me," Anne told me. "She was able to dispose of her children without much thought or emotion, and he followed suit. He disposed of his child."

Another of Jackie's relatives, who asked that I not identify her, told me, "Scott did everything to please his mother so he wouldn't be thrown away. And that's what he did with Laci and Conner. He threw them away."

Anne Bird first met Jackie when she stopped by Jackie's house with her brother Don. Don had contacted her during June 1997 after researching his life history, including birth and adoption records. He had already visited with Jackie and suggested that Anne might like to, also.

Anne noticed that her mother was unusually calm, given that she was meeting a child she had given up decades before. Her initial questions for Anne weren't about how she felt seeing her for the first time, or whether she had been angry at her over the years, or her own angst about the decision she had made to put her up for adoption, they were about whether she liked mushrooms and colorful clothing and who her favorite authors were.

A mother seeing her own flesh and blood after so many years could be expected to stumble a bit, grasping at straws during a first conversation, but Jackie didn't seem nervous at all.

As Anne writes in *Blood Brother*:

Jackie seemed oddly comfortable. . . . I think I wanted her to be at least a little anxious, a little less matter-of-fact. After all, this was the woman who had given me up, and while I didn't expect an apology, I thought some kind of explanation would be nice.

Why didn't Jackie explain? Maybe it was because she didn't feel very badly about what had happened and didn't imagine Anne could feel very badly about it, either. She didn't feel any guilt or worry.

Sound familiar?

According to Anne, one room of the Peterson house was actually arranged like a movie set. Lee Peterson, a fan of the old West, had set up a mock poker game on an old wooden table, with cards actually fanned out in front of each chair. He had placed an antique whiskey bottle with four rusty shot glasses on the table, as if cowboys were hanging out, tying one on. A Civil War uniform was on display.

Tea in the garden. Poker in the den. Neither was real. They were staged. Acts. And most of those present at either seating were ghosts, the living dead.

There was another stark sign that the high emotion Anne was feeling upon meeting her mother wasn't exactly going to be reciprocated. When Jackie took Anne to the antique shop she owned, Anne admired an eighteenth-century beaded embroidery. It wasn't terribly expensive. Less than a hundred dollars. But Jackie didn't give it to the daughter she had abandoned as an infant, the woman who had shown so much personal courage coming to meet her. She told her she would give her a nice discount, then rang up the sale and took the cash.

Anne wasn't comfortable calling Jackie Mom, of course. But the term she and Jackie settled on was all about fantasy.

"How about if I call you my fairy godmother?" Anne suggested.

"Fairy godmother is perfect," Jackie told her. "You'll be my fairy goddaughter."

The sense of unreality only intensified when Anne met her half brother Scott. She found him to be a perfect gentleman, opening doors for her, carrying her bags, pulling out her chair.

She writes:

In retrospect, it all seems a little bit unreal. It may be that my assessment is colored by the horror that came later; I'm not sure. It just seemed a little too studied, a little too perfect. Even when Scott addressed me, he looked right into my eyes, almost as if he knew that it was what you were supposed to do, not realizing that it was perhaps a little too intense.

Scott called Anne Sis right away, which she liked, because she found him charming, at the time.

The only thing that didn't seem perfect about the family she had found, in fact, was the way Jackie Peterson seemed to feel about her future daughter-in-law, Laci. She rolled her eyes at the mention of her name, criticized her clothing, implied she was controlling, an obsessive perfectionist.

Anne got the picture pretty quickly. "No one," she told me, "was good enough for Scott in Jackie's mind. No one was good enough for the Golden Boy."

Chapter 14
MARRIAGE VOWS

Scott and Laci Peterson were married at the Sycamore Mineral Springs Resort before about 150 guests on August 9, 1997. They were surrounded by magnificent flowers. Scott toasted his new in-laws, Sharon and Ron Rocha, and thanked them for their "perfect daughter."

Not everything was perfect, though.

According to the general manager of the resort, Laci's biological father, Dennis Rocha, showed up drunk and needed to be helped into his tuxedo. He had divorced Laci's mother, Sharon, when Laci was just a year old. He and Laci had had a strained relationship for years, seeing each other mostly on holidays.

Maybe Laci's desire to pretty things up, to smile through her pain, to *be* the sunflower tattooed on her ankle, was rooted in the ugliness at home, even before her first birthday. There had to have been unhappiness there from the time she was born, some inkling of the reality that her parents did not love each other, the palpable potential that they would not stay together for long.

Even a one-year-old can feel that kind of discord. And she certainly must have felt sadness and frustration about the absence of her father, year after year, even if she saw him on some weekends and family occasions.

Maybe Laci fantasized that her father would reunite with her mother when she got sick as a little girl, needing surgery to remove an eight-pound tumor from her abdomen. But that didn't happen.

What child wants to focus on that? What little girl wants to dwell on the fact that her father finds anything more compelling than her? Better to tend a secret garden, where she can control what grows, make sure it looks pretty, that no ugly weeds creep in.

The trouble is that life isn't really like a garden. Life always includes some kind of pain, some sort of ugliness. And to the extent we turn our backs on it, we end up facing it, with a vengeance, somewhere down the road.

Maybe if Laci and Scott had been able to talk about what they really shared—innocence lost within the first year of life, the fear of being abandoned, life with a parent trying to obliterate the past (Jackie Peterson using denial and lies; Dennis Rocha perhaps using alcohol), they could have had the beginnings of a real love affair and a real marriage.

That's what a good marriage is, after all. It is never the union of two perfect people who celebrate that perfection the rest of their lives. It is always the union of two people who are imperfect, who have suffered in one way or another (as we all do), and who, if they are very lucky and work very hard at it, can sometimes heal each other.

When they do, we are right to call it true love and to think of it as rare.

Scott and Laci never had a chance at that kind of love. Theirs was a case of the blind leading the blind along a psychological path to oblivion, stretching back over fifty years, to the murder of John Harvey Latham, for about six hundred dollars.

According to Catherine Crier, writing in *A Deadly Game*:

> Amy [Laci's sister] described her sister's relationship with her husband as a good one. The two seemed very much in love, she said. She never heard them argue, and Laci never confided anything negative about Scott to her. She characterized Laci as easily excited, a "talker" who was often "antsy," and "high energy." Scott, however, was calm and relaxed. He never appeared stressed or ruffled, and always seemed "laid-back." . . . She got anything she wanted because Scott tried to give it to her.

Sounds too good to be true.

It was.

Neither Scott Peterson nor Laci Peterson wanted to see the truth or feel pain. Denial was the bond they shared. No other.

While Dennis Rocha was stumbling around before his daughter's wedding reception, trying to get his pants on, Scott was already dressed, having a few drinks at the bar. He chatted up the waitress and pressured her for her phone number. He made sexual comments. The general manager of the resort noted his "inappropriate" behavior.

None of Scott's four half brothers, Mark, Joseph, Don, or John, was standing up for him as his best man. Instead, Scott had chosen someone who hardly knew him, a mere acquaintance named Mike Richardson.

Did Laci worry over that? Did she think of it as peculiar, with Scott having boasted of his perfect family, gathering on weekends for tea in the garden. Or was she simply pleased that the flowers she had chosen to decorate the tables were so beautiful?

Did her mother, Sharon, ask Jackie Peterson for a credible reason Scott was keeping his brothers at a distance, or why they were staying away? Or would a glib one-liner from Jackie like "They're all his best man" have sufficed for her?

Eventually, Laci's biological father got his pants on, though he fell down and split a seam and needed it stapled closed.

Scott got up from his seat at the bar.

Everyone was seated, the music started playing, and Laci emerged in a sleeveless wedding gown, looking perfect. She walked toward her handsome, smiling groom.

The only problem was that neither bride nor groom really knew anything about each other. They were perfect strangers.

Whatever vows Laci and Scott Peterson exchanged that August day, the real promise they made to each other was to keep it that way.

Chapter 15
MARRIED "LIFE"

Scott Peterson's life story, which he had been free to fictionalize before his marriage to Laci, now took an uncomfortable turn toward nonfiction. Long-term relationships are all about reality. The person you live with wakes with you each morning, sleeps with you every night, eats with you, listens to your plans for the future, and can watch whether you follow through on them. What looks like gold from a distance may not glisten when seen up close, day after day. It is much harder to maintain the image of a god or goddess in the eyes of a wife or husband than it is in the eyes of a boyfriend or girlfriend.

But Scott still needed to be the Golden Boy. His mask was all he had. There was nothing but a gaping black hole behind it. He could not risk showing that to anyone, or acknowledging it himself.

Vampires cower before mirrors.

Scott needed to fool himself into continuing to believe he was not only alive but perfect, which meant using his mask of sanity to win the adoration of women, just as he had used it to keep his mother from abandoning him. He needed to have sex with them not just to feel physically present inside his body but to feel chosen, special, worthy of taking his next breath.

Shortly after marrying, Scott and Laci lived apart for a time while she worked in Prunedale, California, in Monterey County and he went to school in Morro Bay, about two hours away by car. Maybe they both needed a little respite from the reality of married life. Maybe they were trying to make good on their wedding vow to remain strangers.

Scott moved in with three roommates and began hosting parties and barbecues with his new buddies.

It was during this time that Scott began his affair with Janet Ilse, a sophomore at Cal Poly, who was six years younger than he. He gave her six dozen roses on their first date and took her to an expensive restaurant. He spoke dreamily of how he planned to succeed in business and earn a fortune.

As he had with his girlfriends during high school, he listened to Janet's every word, laughed at every one of her jokes, professed to have the same tastes in music and art, the same values about religion and family.

Since Janet was a vegetarian, Scott stopped eating meat.

The great mimicker was in rare form.

No doubt Scott felt safe with Janet, adored but not known at all by her, his true self buried deep, well beyond her reach.

He bought her expensive gifts of lingerie and jewelry, went on double dates with her roommate, Tracy, and his own roommate, invited her on romantic getaways, frequently brought his dog McKenzie (a gift from Laci) over to her place, talked about moving in with her, and asked to meet her parents.

I have treated dozens of men and women who have been unfaithful to their spouses. All of them avoided their lovers' family and friends. The anxiety of lying in front of numerous people, never mind the increased risk of being found out, made them want to meet in secret, not at family functions or crowded restaurants.

Scott Peterson didn't feel any of that anxiety. He had shut down that emotion, too.

From *The Mask of Sanity:*

The psychopath [synonymous with sociopath] is nearly always free from minor reactions popularly regarded as "neurotic" or as constituting "nervousness." . . . It is higly typical for him . . . to show a relative immunity from such anxiety and worry as might be judged normal and appropriate in disturbing situations. Regularly we find in him extraordinary poise rather than jitteriness or worry, a smooth sense of physical well-being instead of uneasy preoccupation with bodily functions. Even under concrete circumstances that would for the ordinary person cause embarrassment, confusion, acute insecurity, or visible agitation, his relative serenity is likely to be noteworthy.

Naturally, Scott never invited Janet Ilse to meet his mother or father or siblings. He rarely spoke of them.

The couple had been dating about five months when Janet decided to drop by Scott's place late at night. One of his roommates let her in.

When she opened the door to Scott's bedroom, ready to surprise him with romance, she was shocked to see him lying there with another woman.

The other woman was Laci Peterson, whom Janet would later learn was Scott's wife.

According to Catherine Crier in her book *A Deadly Game:*

> He [Scott] did not move. He did not jump up, or cry out, or beg her forgiveness. He just lay there coolly and stared as she [Janet] lashed out at the two of them. . . . "I'm sorry," was all Scott would say as his roommate burst in and pulled Janet away from the bed.

No empathy. No feelings of guilt. Scott was displaying the hallmarks of sociopathy.

One of the most frightening things about classic sociopaths like Scott Peterson is that they are unmoved by the suffering of others. The terror in a teenage girl's eyes as she is abducted at gunpoint walking home, the tearful begging of a victim about to be dismembered, the panicked struggle against duct tape or ropes binding a victim's wrists and ankles all strike the sociopath as merely interesting, like odd grooming behaviors of an animal at the zoo. At most, they might remind him of something vaguely familiar, a distant memory of his own suffocation, his own destruction. Having buried all fear and sadness himself, he cannot resonate with it in others. It does not move him.

The sociopath, unrestrained by empathy, is free to kill without paying any price emotionally. He will have no flashbacks to the carnage. No lost sleep. No nightmares. He will not turn up in church to ask forgiveness from God.

Generally, as is true for Scott Peterson, the sociopath believes there is no God, that he answers only to himself, no higher authority, that he is his own savior.

One of my patients was a drug dealer and violent criminal named Jimmy who had been horribly abused as a boy. Faced with nearly unbearable suffering, he had shut down emotionally, learning to ignore his grief and panic, even when he was being beaten.

After a while, he didn't experience grief or panic at all.

"I don't understand people who get all bent out of shape when I catch up with them," he told me once. "You cross me, I'm gonna do what I'm gonna do to you whether it freaks you out or not. So what good does it do to lose it?"

"They're frightened of you," I said.

He shrugged, chuckled.

"You wouldn't think of letting someone go because they scream or cry?" I asked him.

"No. I would think of sticking a sock in their mouth."

I nodded. "How about you? Is there anything you're afraid of?"

He shook his head.

"Let's say you were tied up and three men were about to attack you. One of them has a knife. What would you be thinking?"

He pondered that, then nodded to himself.

I thought he might have detected a hint of emotion inside himself. "What would you be thinking?" I asked again.

"I hope they don't cut my eyes out," he said.

"Okay . . ." I couldn't help thinking about what I would be feeling: terror at what was about to happen to me, a particularly intense fear that I might be tortured before being killed, grief that I might never see my family again, rage at the men about to take my life. I would certainly pray.

"Doc?" my patient prompted me.

"Your eyes . . ." I said. "You'd be worried about being blinded?"

"I'd want to be able to keep looking for a way out until they beat me to death," Jimmy said. "And, let me tell you, if I got free, there'd be hell to pay."

Hell to pay, indeed. If Jimmy freed himself his attackers would end up paying for every bit of the hell he had been through, all the way back to his childhood. And here's the really scary part: His pulse wouldn't race. His stomach wouldn't churn. He probably wouldn't even feel much ill-will toward them. He would just be balancing accounts. You thought you had me, but I've got you. Tough luck. No hard feelings.

Scott Peterson would never be able to resonate with the suffering he inflicted on others, either—not the jealousy and rage he provoked in Laci the night Janet Ilse walked into his bedroom, not the sadness and disappointment he caused Janet herself. To him, anyone who had hard feelings about the whole thing would be like someone leaving a movie cinema feeling angry at the villain on screen. It would make no sense. That person didn't really hurt anyone. He doesn't even exist.

Scott probably thought Janet would keep seeing him. When she wouldn't he sought refuge, as was increasingly his habit, in alcohol. But, for sociopaths, drinking can dissolve the mask of sanity that hides the chaos, rage, and perversion behind it. Shortly after Janet broke up with him he got drunk at a bar and began exposing his penis to the crowd. According to Janet, Scott had always worried about the size of his penis and whether he was built well enough to satisfy a woman.

Satisfying women, after all, was one of the only things that made Scott Peterson feel alive.

From *The Mask of Sanity*:

> A major point about the psychopath and his relation to alcohol can be seen in the shocking, fantastic, uninviting, or relatively inexplicable behavior which emerges when he drinks—sometimes when he drinks only a little. . . . Alcohol, as a sort of catalyst, sometimes contributes a good deal to the long and varied series of outlandish pranks and inanely coarse scenes with which nearly every drinking psychopath's story is starred. . . . The alcohol probably does not of itself create such behavior. Alcohol is not likely to bring out any impulse that is not already potential in a personality. . . .

It isn't clear how Laci herself reacted that night. Obviously, she stayed with Scott. Perhaps he told her Janet was obsessed with him since he had dated her back in high school. Maybe he said he had met her at a bar just a few nights before, gotten drunk, and "just kissed" her. Whatever story he spun, she bought it.

Unfazed by his girlfriend walking in on him with his wife, Peterson started a second romance during 1998 with a Cal Poly student named Katy Hansen. Like all his other women, Katy found Scott respectful and attentive, with an aristocratic air. He seemed special. He told her he was single.

The two dated for over two months, including some double dates with their roommates.

Obviously, Scott felt no embarrassment about his behavior, since he was willing to let his roommates in on it. And he had no concern about any potential humiliation he might cause Laci, since he let her spend time with his buddies, who knew that he was routinely cheating on her (and presumably kept his secret).

As he had with Janet Ilse, he continued to bring McKenzie, the dog Laci had given him, on dates with Katy.

He was free again, his mask of sanity a near-perfect fit. He was acting out the role he had down pat: the smiling, clever, confident, regal bachelor.

He was feeling so good he decided to add a few new pages to the script. He told Katy he might travel around the world after graduation, then run for mayor of Fillmore, California, a small city outside Los Angeles.

Sure. Why not politics? Granted, Scott's dreams of being a professional golfer had never materialized. His hopes of pursuing a career in international business had fallen by the wayside. He had no experience in politics at all, nothing real in the way of credentials to recommend him to voters. But none of that mattered. Those were just realities, petty, unwelcome intrusions on his fantasy life. Alone with an adoring woman by his side, he felt all-powerful again, golden, the way his mother Jackie had always made him feel.

The fact that Katy didn't know him well enough to question any of his expansive plans for the future was intoxicating to him. It lifted his feet off the red hot coals of his core grief and rage at having been destroyed, at having no real future. It got him high.

After Katy Hansen watched Laci Peterson place a lei of flowers around Scott's neck and kiss him on the cheek at the Cal Poly graduation ceremony, she told Scott it was over between them.

Scott didn't understand why she should be so upset. He sent her a dozen pink roses.

Katy never contacted him.

That wouldn't have stopped Scott Peterson from reaching out to Katy in the future had he not found other women to help distract him from the distant, gnawing sense that he was dead inside. The fact that she might find it bizarre to get a phone call or three dozen roses or some yummy cookies tied up with a bow from him, out of the blue, six months or a year in the future, wouldn't bother him at all. It wouldn't be about what she felt, if he could even guess at that, it would be about what he needed from her. It would be about the distance from his feelings of complete and utter emptiness, from the gaping, black hole behind his mask of sanity, that her saying "Yes, you can come by. Yes, you are special. Yes, I adore you" could take him.

It would be about the lifeblood she could transfuse him with.

Chapter 16
NEW LIFE

Laci had moved back in with Scott in San Luis Obispo while he was busy romancing Katy Hansen. She had apparently forgiven him for his affair with Janet Ilse, just as she had forgiven him for humiliating her at the Pacific Café where she had come face-to-face with his lover Lauren Putnat, then fled to the rest room in tears.

Many women would not have stuck around after either indiscretion. But Laci wanted to keep things looking pretty. She would have tried very hard to accept any explanation her charming husband could serve up that would allow her to believe her marriage wasn't a wreck. She would have used denial to blind herself to all the ugly realities.

When Laci was a child, her father had walked out on her and her mother. She would do anything she could to avoid believing she was losing another's man's heart.

Laci eventually took a job as a banquet coordinator at the Sycamore Springs Resort, where her wedding had taken place. Scott started working with his father, Lee, who made him a partner in his crating business.

Over time, each of them grew dissatisfied with their jobs. They decided to pursue a dream of theirs and open a restaurant. They renovated a vacant building near the Cal Poly campus into The Shack, a hamburger joint that became a favorite of undergraduates.

Like everything else Scott Peterson had tried, however, the reality of running a restaurant didn't match his fantasies. It was a lot of work. Employees were tough to find and tough to manage. Customers had to be catered to.

Laci and Scott sold the place, though it isn't clear they netted much, if any, profit.

Scott wasn't turning out to be the provider Laci probably imagined he would be, given all his dreams of wealth and power.

The couple moved in with Laci's parents for a while, then accepted a $30,000 gift from Jackie and Lee Peterson for the down-payment on a $177,000 fixer-upper on Covena Avenue in the dusty city of Modesto, where Laci grew up.

Buying the house had to be a bitter pill for Scott Peterson.

Modesto is no San Luis Obispo, certainly no Rancho Santa Fe (where Lee and Jackie had leveraged a fake life, including a Ferrari and Rolls-Royce). It is working class, not aristocratic.

According to Anne Bird, Scott's living in Modesto clearly didn't sit well with Jackie Peterson. She thought it was on the wrong side of the tracks. She told Anne, "They're not going to be staying in that town for the rest of their lives."

Lauren Putnat, one of Scott's former girlfriends, told me, "I think Scott must have resented the move to Modesto. It wouldn't go with what he was aiming for—living in a bigger city and having adventures and money and all that. When I first heard where he had ended up, I was shocked. I couldn't picture him living there at all."

Scott ended up taking a job about as far from being a professional golfer or an international businessman or mayor of Fillmore, California, as you can get. He started work for Tradecorp, selling fertilizer and other agricultural products to farms and flower growers.

Scott would making his "living" helping spread waste material over flowers to help them grow.

Despite that psychological poetry, the Tradecorp job wasn't exactly poetry for Scott financially. The company was based in Spain and just getting established on the West Coast of the United States. They were struggling.

The Golden Boy was losing his shine.

He wasn't so special, after all.

His parents did what they could to keep reality at bay, buying him a golf membership to a country club for $25,000 and fronting him money to put a pool in his backyard, but Laci had to get a job as a substitute teacher to help make ends meet.

Then real life dealt the fantasy existence of Scott Peterson a devastating blow. Laci had been trying to conceive a child for two years with no luck. Scott probably assumed she couldn't have a baby, partly due to the surgery she had had as a little girl to remove a massive tumor (surgery which had included removing one of her fallopian tubes). But that wasn't *true*. One day, Laci called him and told him she was pregnant.

In a rare moment of candor, Scott would later tell Rosemarie Rocha, Laci's sister-in-law, "I was kind of hoping for infertility."

Maybe, after getting the call from Laci, he had the fleeting thought he should call his mother, send her on another mission like the one she had gone on to Arizona, to convince his "lover" to have an abortion. But this was his wife. Even Jackie might not understand. How could she keep seeing her son as the Golden Boy if he were to urge his wife to abort their first child?

Maybe Jackie wanted a grandchild. Maybe that was the reason Scott had gotten married to begin with. Maybe that was the reason she and Lee had ponied up the down payment for Scott's house. They had decided it was time for him to start a family.

They had decided.

He hadn't decided anything. Ever.

He felt completely and utterly alone.

He had always known deep in his heart, in the tiny space he had never surrendered to Jackie or Lee, that there was no one in the world he could rely on other than himself. He had no real friends. He never let his parents know he even existed.

He had never sought strength from God, either. Because at core, God is about the immeasurable connections between people. And Scott Peterson was connected to nothing and no one. To him, God was a lie told by weak people who wanted to believe in myths like the soul.

He sat with the uncomfortable knowledge that Laci was pregnant only a minute before fixing his mask of sanity firmly in place, again. He called Laci back and told her, with all the manufactured joy he could muster, that he was canceling all his meetings, that he was rushing home to see her, that he just couldn't wait to touch her stomach and feel their baby kicking.

That sounded good to him. It sounded like the kind of thing a husband with a pregnant wife might do.

It sounded good to Laci, too.

Chapter 17
BIRTH EQUALS DEATH

For men infinitely better equipped psychologically than Scott Peterson, having a child can cause severe anxiety. Men feel they must say loudly and frequently how excited they are to become fathers, but in the privacy of my office, many also frequently admit how frightened they are. Some tell me that they wish their wives or girlfriends had never become pregnant. A few even admit, in tears, that they wish something would "happen" to the baby.

Becoming a father can shake the psychological foundation of even well-adjusted men. But they can't tell anyone what is happening inside them. The subject is taboo. With all the celebration around him, a future father has no one to talk to about his doubts. His wife would be hurt to know he had any. He can't even turn to his own father, who would be loath to divulge any second thoughts he might have had bringing a child into the world, given that his child is the one asking the question.

You might think a man's friends would listen to his worries. But amongst men there is a conspiracy of silence on this topic. The moment we hear the news that someone's wife or partner is going to have a baby, words like "congratulations," "awesome" and "fantastic" roll off our tongues.

We create a tidal wave of celebration, big enough to drown out any other emotion.

We aren't about to ask a buddy, "So, how do you feel about it, man? Did you really want a kid?" If we did, we might get asked the same question ourselves.

Many men who are not normally superstitious, believe that expressing anything but elation about becoming fathers could actually cause their wives to lose their babies, that God or nature or the universe could punish them for their ambivalence.

With all the increased equality between men and women, impending fatherhood is a time when men feel called upon to appear more certain of ourselves than ever, more confident of our abilities to earn a living, more in love with our wives or girlfriends.

But we may not feel that way.

I certainly didn't. In addition to real joy when I learned my wife was pregnant with our first child, I felt that I was moving into a whole new stage of my life, one that I knew nothing about and that seemed as though it would be extremely challenging. I didn't know if I would make a good father. I didn't know whether having a family would still leave me time to be a writer and a psychiatrist. And, as much as I loved my wife, I remember thinking that having a child with her would make it nearly impossible for me to rationalize leaving her, even if we one day fell out of love.

Even more than getting married or purchasing our home, having a child together seemed to be a permanent bond. Inescapable.

I remember visiting my own psychiatrist, the late Dr. James Mann, then already over eighty, and telling him that my wife was pregnant.

He smiled and nodded. "Okay," he said. "Let's have it."

"What?" I smiled back.

"How do you feel?"

"Good, great. I mean, I just hope it's healthy and . . ."

"Clichés. I've heard them all. Tell me the rest."

"The rest?" I stalled.

"Don't bullshit me, Keith," he said. "I'm eighty-two years old. I've heard just about everything there is to hear. And I have kids myself. Just tell me the truth."

That session ended up running overtime.

More than one of my male patients have confessed to me that they worry their wives will become so involved with their babies that they will lose all interest in them.

A number tell me they are petrified to be present in the delivery room, where they fear they will feel useless and helpless.

Some worry that their wives will no longer want to have sex, or will experience pain during sex.

Some fear they will no longer be sexually attracted to their wives, given the changes in their bodies.

And it turns out that the ways pregnancy affects female anatomy are still mysterious to even very intelligent men. A few of my patients, including a psychologist and a hospital CEO, have had the courage to ask me, as a physician, what will happen to their wives' vaginas when babies pass through their birth canals, whether they will "go back to the way they were before."

They fear that they will never again be able to attain sexual satisfaction during intercourse.

"You don't want to run this one by the chief of OB/Gyn at your hospital?" I asked the CEO.

He laughed. "That's not something I would ever bring up with someone I work with," he told me. "I barely found the courage to ask you."

Still other men have told me they worry that having a child will be the end of them being attractive to women other than than their wives. They'll be seen as "family men," not *men*. And it isn't that they necessarily want to have affairs. Most just want to be sure that they won't be written off by the opposite sex—ignored, unseen.

They don't want to lose the energy that they still derive from flirting with women or being admired by them.

Several patients of mine about to be fathers have found themselves confronting raw emotions about their relationships with their own fathers, including disappointment and anger. Some, with particularly fractured relationships with their dads, pray for daughters, certain they will fail at fathering boys when they weren't well fathered themselves.

"I can do the little-girl thing," one of them, named Tom, told me. "I think girls are awesome. But I don't know how I feel about boys."

"Including yourself," I said.

"What do you mean?" he asked.

"You told me before that you're not sure your dad ever really loved you."

Tom's eyes filled up.

"You're not sure you'll love your son," I told him. "But that's only because you've never seen it done—or felt it done."

Any or all these issues can come to life in a man's psyche when his wife or girlfriend tells him that she is pregnant. They can feel overwhelming. For a few men, they can feel like the end of the world.

That probably explains why, according to findings published in the *Journal of the American Medical Association*, **the leading cause of death in pregnant women is murder**.

Statistics show that of every 1,000 pregnant women, 170 are

assaulted by their partners during the last five months of pregnancy.

A one-year study by *The Washington Post* of violent deaths across America disclosed that, during the past fourteen years, 1,367 pregnant women and new mothers were murdered.

That's almost two pregnant women murdered in the United States every week.

Scott Peterson was in the middle of the perfect psychological storm.

He had been raised by a mother who had rid herself of two children and who had considered giving away a third. For her, becoming pregnant had always triggered abandonment by a lover she craved, the end of romance, the end of love.

Scott himself had been removed from his mother immediately after birth, placed in a plastic oxygen tank where he had had to fight for every breath. There was no warmth associated with coming into the world, only quiet desperation.

He had gone home with a mother who had proceeded to suffocate him psychologically, to strangle everything that was uniquely *him*, to gold plate her trophy son, and entomb him in her vision of him as the perfect child.

For Scott Peterson, birth equaled death.

He had for many years used the adoration of women and his ability to penetrate them to remind himself that he existed at all, that he had any effective power in the world. And he knew that with a child, it would be harder to make the moves he was used to making—harder to travel, harder to disappear and cheat.

He would be anchored to a family, and all that "family" reminded him of was his own soul murder.

His sex life, the only life he had ever known, was under attack—by a woman, his wife, soon to be a mother. Like his mother.

He had been utterly defenseless in the face of Jackie's insistence that he suffocate himself to death. He had been a child.

Now he was an adult. Now he could finally defend himself.

Since he had never been able to truly feel for another human being (and had never let himself feel for himself), none of the joy of new life registered with him. He saw no potential gain offsetting what he considered his unquestionable losses.

Everything Scott Peterson had used to sustain his vision of

himself as special and worthy and alive was crashing down around him. He wasn't on the PGA tour. He played at a local country club he couldn't really afford, walking the course with his aging father, the man who had shoved a golf club in his hand when he was just five years old and told him to use it. His job was mundane, and he wasn't even particularly good at it. His house was modest, in a dead-end, dusty town called Modesto.

Now that home would not just have a woman inside it, a wife intent on tending a pretty garden and keeping Scott in her life at any cost. It would have a wife *and mother and a baby* inside it.

Scott would be going home every night to *a house with a mother and a baby inside it*, the very sort of place where he was spiritually murdered.

Back to the scene of the crime.

Birth equals death.

And Laci was talking about wanting a bigger house, big enough for more children. She had reportedly inquired with a realtor about finding a home in the $400,000 to $600,000 range.

To Scott, it would be nothing more than a fine casket.

Sharon Rocha, Laci's mother, confided in me that she wonders whether Scott had been trying to cause Laci to abort Conner before he killed her daughter. "I think he may have been trying to cause a miscarriage," she said. "There were strange symptoms in the weeks before he murdered my daughter. And if he had achieved that, I wonder if Laci would still be here. Because if he could have gotten rid of the baby, he would have had the life he had before."

For Scott Peterson, with every week of Laci's pregnancy, every inch her belly grew to make way for new life, the tiny pipe sticking up through the soil covering his grave would feel as if it were filling with more and more earth. He might sometimes literally feel as though he could not get any air into his lungs, that he could not move his arms or legs, that he was being crushed.

He might pull his truck over to the side of the road, certain he was about to die.

Occasionally he might even check the rearview mirror, thinking he was being followed, that someone was out to get him, to do him in.

He would drink more than ever, but never be able to buy himself more than an hour or two of freedom, a little time outside the family prison he was born into, a chance for his demons to come out and play. Maybe he exposed himself again. Maybe he masturbated, thinking about the kinds of fantasies that really excited him—being restrained during sex, choked, dehumanized.

But reality would keep meeting him in the night, trying to break into his consciousness.

Because the truth always wins.

You can't outrun it.

He might wake from sleep, screaming, groping at his groin, certain he had been castrated, that he would never have sex again.

He might find himself weeping silently, and be at a loss as to why. Doubting his tears were even real, he might touch them, then look in disbelief at his wet fingertips.

He might wonder whether he was going insane.

And he would never stumble on the fact that he always had been.

Desperate for relief, he would go out again and again looking for fixes of the lifeblood he craved, transfusions from women— flirtations, phone sex, groping, one-night stands, whatever he could get.

He would put on fine clothes, comb his hair, check his smile in the mirror.

Just when everyone thought they had him cornered, he would tell himself, he would find a way out, a way to feel special again, a way to breathe.

And then, on November 20, 2002, it happened. He found himself looking at a woman who made him feel more than special. She made him feel like a knight in shining armor, a god.

She made him feel like gold again.

Chapter 18
AMBER

She was blond and beautiful, and she was a single mother with one child, just like his own mother, Jackie, had been when she had met his father, Lee.

Her name was Amber Frey, a massage therapist from Madera, California, about ninety miles south of Modesto.

Scott had met Amber's best friend, Shawn Sibley, while he was having a few drinks at a business convention in Anaheim a month earlier.

Sibley was in a committed relationship, so he didn't waste much time trying to seduce her. He told her he was single and "looking for someone he could spend the rest of his life with." He was sick of "bimbos," and wanted to be with someone intelligent.

He explained he was from Sacramento, but kept an office in Modesto. His work took him all over the world.

Despite Scott joking (with a little alcohol in him) that he should write "horny bastard" on his business card to get dates, Sibley thought he might be a good catch for her best friend. The next day she asked Amber whether it would be all right to give Scott her number.

Amber agreed.

Scott waited several weeks to call her, then invited her out to dinner.

The two met at a place called the Elephant Bar, then returned to Scott's hotel so he could shower and change.

According to Amber Frey's book *Witness: For the Prosecution of Scott Peterson*, Scott changed into a blue shirt and black pants that matched Amber's blue top and black skirt. He was a very, very good mimicker.

He and Laci had the same cute habit. They wore matching outfits to Scott's long-lost half sister, Anne Bird's, wedding.

True to form, Scott had packed Champagne and fresh strawberries in his luggage for Amber so they could toast their first date.

Everything was perfectly scripted.

They went out to dinner at an intimate Japanese restaurant, ate in a private room, and talked about their lives.

Scott's mask of sanity was pristine. He listened intently to Amber as she told him about her work as a massage therapist. He asked her what she liked about it, how difficult it was, the different kinds of clients she had. He frowned at all the right times, nodded at all the right times, laughed at all the right times.

He was simply doing what he had learned to do growing up. Possessed of the knowledge that he could be abandoned at any time, sensing that expressing any true feelings could lead him to lose the only people who said they loved him, "living" in a perpetual state of panic, he had learned to monitor every facial expression of his mother and father, the most subtle change in their tones of voice, any shift in their moods. Whatever he detected, he responded to instantly, denying his own sadness when they seemed happy, laughing when they seemed to enjoy a joke, disliking anyone they did, adopting every one of their ideas, pretending they were his own, then actually believing they were.

He was a textbook example of the "subtly constructed reflex machine" Hervey Cleckley described in *The Mask of Sanity*.

He seemed genuinely moved by the fact that Amber had had troubled relationships with men in the past, including one that had left her as a single parent raising her twenty-month-old daughter, Ayiana. She told him that she herself was from a broken home; her parents Ron and Brenda divorced when she was five years old.

Scott said he lived alone and traveled constantly, to Europe and Africa. He loved animals but had no pets because he wasn't around enough to take care of them. He told her he wanted to settle down with the right person.

Amber was smitten. The way Scott looked at her made her feel as if she *were* the right person.

The couple went to a karaoke bar where they drank more. Then they bought a bottle of gin and drank even more. Then they went back to Scott's room and had sex.

In bed, he was even more attentive, more expert at adjusting to what his lover wanted him to do, what she wanted him to be.

Amber started kissing his chest, so he unbuttoned his shirt. She moved her mouth lower, so he unbuttoned his pants. She looked up at him, so he reached down for her, brought her to her feet. She closed her eyes, so he kissed her. She turned her face ever so slightly toward the ceiling, so he caressed her neck. She pressed against him, so he moved his knee between her legs. When she let her knees fall wider apart, he ran his hand up her thigh.

The sex was all about Amber—what she wanted and needed. Scott seemed to have a sixth sense where she wanted to be touched and kissed. He was like a sex toy she operated by mental remote control, just by thinking, without having to lift a finger.

Amber must have thought the sex was extraordinary. This man *knew* what she liked. It would have taken her much longer, perhaps as long as it took Lauren Putnat, to realize there was something repetitive and boring and unnerving about the way he made "love," that she was sleeping with someone who never let on what *he* liked, never took control, never let her see *him*, only his anatomy.

She was sleeping with a dead man.

The next day Scott told Amber he had meetings to get to. He called later in the day and tried to see her, but she had to work and was already exhausted.

He promised to visit her after he was back from his "hunting trip to Alaska."

He drove home to Modesto.

Laci probably noticed her husband seemed in an especially good mood. He might even have asked to touch her belly again, to try to feel their baby kicking. Maybe he asked her to go shopping for furniture for the baby's room. He felt better, as if he could breathe, as if he were just visiting his home life, not actually condemned to live it.

He felt free again.

As the days passed, he drank up Amber's adoration on the phone, reveled in the role he was playing as her savior. He called her December 2 and told her he was back from Alaska and near her apartment. The two of them picked Ayiana up at school and went on a pleasant hike to Squaw's Leap, in nearby Auberry, California.

Scott was all prepared. He even had a blanket for the three of them.

"He seemed very happy," Amber writes in *Witness*. "He couldn't stop grinning at me and Ayiana.

Then he told her the truth for the first time, even though it sounded as if he had misspoken. "Look at me," he said. "I've got a rigor-mortis smile." A cadaver's smile.

Later, he gave Ayiana a gift he had brought for her and then cooked dinner for the whole fake family, the only kind Scott had ever lived with, the only kind he *could* live with.

Dinner was perfect. Laci's hero Martha Stewart would have been proud.

Scott and Amber ended up in bed again.

Amber writes:

> I felt unusually comfortable around Scott, as if I'd known him for a very long time. I didn't feel I had to try to be anyone other than who I was, and it seemed as if he felt very much the same way. In a word, being with Scott was effortless.

There was a reason for that. Being with Scott would be like being with your shadow. You kind of figure it'll stick real close and go where you do.

Effortless. Like magic.

You seem sad, Scott is sad with you. You're happy, there he is, smiling his big rigor-mortis smile.

Unlike talking to a real person with his own ideas and intuitions, who might even disagree with your views, who might look bored now and then, who might have had a bad day and show it, everything you think and feel strikes a cord with him. He is flawless.

He likes exactly what you like in bed.

He wants the same things from life.

You have never met someone with whom you have so much in common.

Because you are actually alone, sitting by yourself, talking to yourself.

It was effortless for Amber Frey to be with Scott Peterson because he wasn't really there.

Chapter 19
"TRUE LOVE"

Something strange began to happen inside Scott's mind. As he spent more time with Amber and Ayiana, as he talked more with Amber on the phone, he began to think he was actually in love with her.

Nothing could be further from the truth, but cozying up to the truth wasn't part of Scott's repertoire.

What he interpreted as love was—initially, at least—nothing more than relief. Amber represented freedom from reality, the opportunity to be "shiny" again. Golden. She was his refuge from the facts of life: that he couldn't earn much of a living, that he lived in a modest home in Modesto, that his dad had had to front him not only his downpayment but his membership fee at the golf club and the money to build a pool in his backyard, that he was married to someone who was substitute teaching to help pay the mortgage, that his wife was about to become a mother, that she would start loving someone else (Conner), that she might stop working, that she wanted a bigger house and would probably get pregnant again, that he would have to work harder to support a family he didn't even want, that he might fail at it, that he would have to be home more than he could stand.

None of that existed in Amber's mind, so, when Scott was with her, none of it existed for him.

With Amber, he actually *was* the successful international businessman he had talked about becoming. He was single, a great catch.

Perfect.

To Scott, Amber was, at the beginning, just another Jackie—adoring him, so long as he didn't let her know anything about him.

It must have felt like enough to keep the rigor-mortis smile on his face, forever.

But there was something else happening, something very subtle, yet very powerful. Amber was talking to Scott a great deal about her feelings, including her disappointments in life. She was a highly emotional and honest person who was willing to look at the broken parts of her existence and let him see them, too. She was trusting him with her heart. Her truth.

Amber and her sister, Ava, had been shuttled between her father's house and her mother's house after her parents divorced. She then lived exclusively with her mother for a time. Then her mother met another man, and brought her daughters to live with him. But that only lasted a few years. When it ended abruptly, Amber, Ava, and their mother moved to an apartment. But then, the very next year, Amber's mother met yet another man and married him. So Amber and Ava (for a reason that remains unclear) moved in with their dad in the mountains at Yosemite Springs Parkway. Then their dad got married to a woman who Amber recalls as "odd," who kept to herself and ignored the family. That marriage didn't last either.

Amber's life had been a mess.

This was a woman who was just trying to hold herself together, not trying to be Martha Stewart. She wasn't another Jackie. Not even close. She had loose ends in her life and wasn't trying to hide them—at least she wasn't doing a very good job of it.

As a massage *therapist* she was literally in touch with people's pain. People came to her and talked about their lives as she laid hands on them. And she was good at what she did. Some of her clients became her friends.

She was a healer.

She seemed to truly want to know who Scott was. And she seemed strong, spiritually grounded and trustworthy, as though maybe she could handle it.

When Amber eventually asked whether Scott wanted children of his own, in fact, he told her he didn't. He wanted to have a vasectomy (translation: to sever his connection to birth, which for him represented death) even though he was only thirty years old. He took a risk and let her inside his head that little bit. He told her things could be perfect with the two of them and little Ayiana.

He was actually letting himself be known, dropping his mask, if only for a split second.

It was rare.

For him, it must have been one of the only times in his entire existence when he felt as if he could really breathe.

And when Amber didn't tell him that a vasectomy would be a deal breaker, when she listened to him and asked more about his feelings and shared her own, he may have felt something more for her than he had ever felt for any human being. It is not beyond the realm of possibility that he felt something close to love—no mere transfusion from a woman but an actual thawing of his own lifeblood, a crack in the walls he had built around his soul. He told her she was beautiful, inside and outside.

He may actually have meant it.

People have the power to heal one another.

As the author Joseph Campbell has written: "One thing that comes out in myths is that at the bottom of the abyss comes the voice of salvation. The black moment is the moment when the real message of transformation is going to come. At the darkest moment comes the light."

But it wasn't to be.

Chapter 20
REALITY

On December 6, 2002, reality swept like a tidal wave into Scott Peterson's fantasy life.

That day, Amber Frey's friend Shawn Sibley mentioned Scott's name to a colleague of hers, a man named Feras Almassari. Almassari had actually once interviewed for a job with Tradecorp, where Scott worked, and had met him.

Scott had told Almassari that he was independently wealthy and had moved to the United States from Europe to launch the company. He told him he had so much money lying around that his wife hadn't even shopped around before grabbing a house in Modesto.

Shawn couldn't believe it was the same Scott Peterson, but Almassari felt certain.

Minutes later, Shawn phoned Scott and reached him.

According to Amber, the conversation went this way:

"Tell me I didn't set my best friend up on a date with a married man!" Sibley said, fuming.

"What?" Scott asked.

"I just got off the phone with someone who says he knows you. He says you're married and live in Modesto."

"That's crazy," Scott said. "It must be another Scott Peterson."

Shawn told Scott she didn't believe him and would find out the truth.

In a way, though, Scott had been honest with her. It *was* another Scott Peterson, of course, who had romanced Amber. It was the single, wealthy international businessman who carried Champagne and strawberries with him on first dates and cooked elaborate dinners for her and her little girl.

Shawn searched Sacramento County records on the Web and found what she was looking for: Peterson was married and lived in Modesto, just as Almassari had told her.

She called Scott back and confronted him with the information.

He broke down in tears and told her he *had* been married.

"Are you currently married?" she demanded.

"I lost my wife," he said, sobbing. He told her the subject was still hard to talk about. He hadn't fully dealt with his grief.

There was a kernel of truth to that statement, too. Scott had kept *all* his grief, about his entire existence, at bay for a very long time. And no doubt, he did believe at some level that he had lost Laci, that she was already with another Golden Boy, the truly innocent child named Conner growing inside her.

Once Laci gave birth, Scott might have believed that it would be completely over between them. He would no longer be the object of her affection. She would no longer worship him.

He promised Shawn he would tell Amber about his prior marriage.

She agreed to let him speak for himself.

Peterson felt as though he were drowning again. His freedom to re-create himself, to be reborn, to *breathe*, was being choked off by stubborn facts. His marriage. Impending fatherhood. Increasing financial obligations to a family. Mortgage payments on a house that was an embarrassment to him.

He was being killed. Again.

He was about to lose his lifeline to freedom—Amber, and everything she represented. Sex, of course, but also safety and adoration.

I believe Scott thought he loved her chiefly because she was helping him escape reality at a critical time. He was clinging to her like a child carried out of a burning house. But I also believe that she had reached him, had actually touched the little boy inside him, cowering deep in a smoke-filled room inside his own soul, terrified to stay, terrified to leave, terrified even to be found.

In another piece of psychological poetry (which I cannot resist), note what Amber is in nature: a fossil resin that often embraces dead organisms, that when rubbed can sometimes literally spark with energy. It is believed by many to be an amulet with the power to ignite true love.

Scott Peterson knew one thing for sure: Amber would not stay with him if he were married. She had made it plain how she felt about married men cavorting with other women.

What Scott may or may not have known was that Amber had once had a romance with another man whose wife was about to deliver a child. That man, named Steve, had told her he was in love with her and that he wanted to spend his life with her. Amber moved in with him and helped support him emotionally through his wife's pregnancy and promised to include his child in their lives forever.

But some number of months after his wife delivered, Steve left Amber *and* his wife, moved to Las Vegas, and married someone else.

The relationship caused Amber severe emotional suffering. It was the primary reason she sought support in the Church.

Gloria Allred, Amber's attorney, told me: "Amber is very black-and-white now on issues like that. There is no chance she would have stayed with Scott Peterson if he told her he had a wife, with a child on the way. It would have been completely out of the question."

This, of course, was Scott Peterson's earliest and deepest fear—that letting himself be known would result in his abandonment.

He had felt that terror with Jackie. Now he felt it again.

Had it been otherwise, Laci and Conner might be alive today. If by some miracle Scott had felt free enough to tell Amber Frey his whole truth, safe enough in her love to believe that she would stick with him through the birth of his son, that she would forget the past and again be forgiving enough to quietly plan a way for the two of them to be together at some point in the future, I do not believe he would have murdered anyone.

He would have known unconditional love for the first time. I believe it would have been irresistible to him.

Three lives would have been saved. Laci's, Conner's, and Scott's.

But Scott knew for sure that that was not going to happen.

Amber had already been there, done that.

Three days later, on December 9, Scott purchased the fishing boat he would use to dump the body of his pregnant wife and unborn child in the San Francisco Bay.

Then he went to see Amber.

Amber recalled the visit for police this way. I have italicized recollections of hers that I consider particularly important:

". . . he was very upset, very distraught about something he had done that was very devastating possibly to a beau-

tiful relationship . . . and he said . . . it'd be so much easier if you just hated me and you didn't wanna see me
again, and I'd understand and, and . . . I just hate myself
so much right now. . . . *Then he talked to me about lying*
and then he goes I just . . . had such a horrible weekend
this week and it wasn't fun for anybody 'cause I had this
on my mind and I was like, What?! You know, and I'm
holding his hand and *he was crying, his stomach kept*
churning and he was having trouble swallowing and tears
were pouring out of his eyes. And he said, *I lied to you*
about being, you asked me if I'd been married and I have,
but it's . . . in my past and it's so hard for me, because I
just, I've had such a hard time dealing with . . . and uh I
said okay. And . . . I'm thinking well she's passed away
you know. . . .

Scott was having trouble getting the words out. Amber com-
forted him:

". . . I go I'm sorry this was so hard for you to tell me and
I thank you for sharing this with me. And, and I . . . there
will be a time for you, you know, to share more and he's
like . . . *taking breaths and he's having trouble swallowing.*
He's like . . . you're not mad and I said how can I be mad
if something, you know, is . . . how can I possibly for . . .
that's understandable if you have a loss. . . . And he goes,
and, and he said uh this will be the first holidays without
her. . . ."

As she writes in her book *Witness,* Amber asked Scott
whether he was ready for a relationship with her.

"God, yes!" he replied.

Scott Peterson may have been a good actor. He was certainly
the "subtly constructed reflex machine" wearing a "mask of sanity" that Hervey Cleckley described in his landmark work on sociopathy. But I do not believe he could have faked every iota of
what Amber Frey described—the breathlessness, the tears
streaming down his face, the difficulty swallowing, the stunning
admission that he had lied to her in the past.

I do not think it was purely an act when he asked her whether she could forgive him for omitting the death of his wife (which was truly about to happen) from the life story he had told her.

In a way, he may have been making sure he could have her once Laci really was dead, that he hadn't already lost her.

I am not even sure whether he was lying when he told her—and God—that he truly wanted a relationship with her.

I think he may actually have been telling the truth, for once in his life.

Chapter 21
LIVING HELL

As Scott was planning to kill Laci and Conner, he continued to romance Amber Frey. He did so at some peril to himself. It would have been much safer for him to put space and time between his affair and his crime.

But Scott didn't want to lose contact with Amber. He was, at minimum, addicted to her. He may well have believed he loved her. She represented freedom not only from his marriage and the impending demands of fatherhood but from the internal prison to which he had been sentenced in childhood.

Scott attended two parties with Amber on December 11 and December 14. The first was a birthday party for Shawn Sibley's fiancé, the second a Christmas formal. He brought her roses. He posed for photos with her. He made her her favorite childhood snack—a Pink Lady caramel apple. He made love with her. He told her she could consider him her boyfriend.

After learning that her daugher, Ayiana, had taken a fall one day, he came to the house and changed the little girl's bandage.

He asked Amber how she had *felt* earlier in the day, when the accident had happened. "It must be incredibly hard to see your daughter in pain," he said.

I think he really wanted to know. As a stranger to our world, a man cut off for decades from all genuine emotions, he had found a woman at one with them, and willing to share them.

He had to have her.

He felt as though his life depended on it.

On December 15 he told Amber he was leaving to go on a business trip to New Mexico and Arizona. The two of them talked briefly on December 16, December 19, and December 21. During that time, Scott was actually at home in Modesto, buying supplies, including a fishing rod and reel, to go with the boat he had purchased December 9. He applied for and received a fishing license. At some point, he made the anchors he would use to weight down Laci's body.

As a sociopath, he would rationalize what he was about to do. He would feel no guilt.

Who could blame him for defending himself? It was Laci and Conner or him.

There was no other way. He had to have Amber.

Even if all his instincts were wrong, even if he somehow could convince Amber to stay with him after admitting he was married and that his wife was pregnant, Laci and Conner would be left alone, abandoned—a young mother and her infant son, unloved and unwanted.

That was Jackie's story; Laci would be better off dead than repeating it. Translation: My mother would have been better off dead. I would have been better off never having been born.

And, taking that line of thought just one more unconscious step: *Laci equals Jackie. I am killing my mother, aborting myself, finally setting everything right, finally telling the whole truth. Only by doing all this can I be truly reborn.*

On December 22, Scott called and told Amber he was back in Sacramento, on his way to Maine to go duck hunting, before jetting off to Europe. He would be gone a month.

When Amber mentioned that it would be a good time for her to start taking the pill again, Scott told her not to bother, that he would go forward with his vasectomy. Despite her having told him that she wanted more children, he was willing to tell the truth, even if it disappointed her. "Ayiana is enough for me," he said. "I would raise her as my own."

When Lee met Jackie Peterson, after all, she had only one child (John). And, deep in Scott's psyche, he believed his parents should have left well enough alone. They should have spared him the living hell, the relentless strangulation of his soul, that he had known for thirty years.

Finally, all that would be over. He would destroy the past and re-create himself.

From *The Book of Job*, translated by Stephen Mitchell:

God damn the day I was born and the night that forced me from the womb. On that day—let there be darkness; let it never have been created; let it sink back into the void. Let chaos overpower it; let black clouds overwhelm it; let the sun be plucked from the sky.

Chapter 22
REBIRTH

In the hours before 5:17 P.M., December 24, when Scott Peterson called his mother-in-law, Sharon Rocha, and told her Laci was "missing," he murdered her, weighted down her body, and dumped it in the San Francisco Bay.

No murder weapon was ever found. The autopsies performed on Laci and Conner could not establish a cause of death.

As a forensic psychiatrist, I think the pieces of the puzzle fit together best this way. There is, of course, no way to definitively prove my theory:

- The large mag light that Scott Peterson brought with him to Anne Bird's house (and which later disappeared) was, quite possibly, the murder weapon. Scott no doubt had heard how his grandfather was killed in his salvage yard—struck with a length of rusty pipe. I believe that image never left him and directed his choice of what to use to initially render Laci unconscious— fifty-seven years later, very nearly to the day.

- Given Scott's history of being psychologically suffocated, along with Anne Bird's report that he obsessively cleaned the pool at his home on more than one occasion after Laci went missing, it is possible that he struck Laci while she lounged in the pool to relieve the pain in her back (as was her habit in the later months of pregnancy), then held her under the water, drowning her. This would also be thematically consistent with his plan to eventually dispose of her body in the waters of the San Francisco Bay.

Water, of course, is powerfully connected to themes of both birth and death.

That's a guess—my best guess—at how the crime took place.

But what was happening inside Scott Peterson's mind as he murdered Laci and Conner?

As a person imitating a person, one of the living dead, I believe Peterson was probably eerily efficient at killing. He had planned everything. He would do what was required of him to take his wife's life, never losing control. He would not feel nervous. His pulse would stay dead even. His energies would be focused on proceeding with his plan step-by-step, trying to avoid leaving behind any evidence.

He would not shed a tear. He had wept at the thought of saying good-bye to Amber, but she was a woman he wanted. She represented freedom. Laci was a woman he no longer wanted. She represented his enslavement.

As he held Laci underwater, he would feel nothing. If she struggled against him, he would not be moved. He would be annoyed. He would only grow more resolute, only feel stronger.

So much of his developing psyche, including his sexuality while growing up in Jackie's house, was focused on coping with his own spiritual annihilation that he may well have been sexually stimulated by the act of murder. It is even possible he achieved climax as he delivered Laci and his unborn child out of this world.

He felt more powerful in that moment than he had ever felt in his existence.

He was finally telling the truth. He was finally stepping out from behind his mask of sanity.

In his mind, he had not only killed Laci, he had killed his mother. He had erased the past.

Everything must have looked new to him. The water felt cool. His skin tingled. The colors around him were suddenly more vibrant. He could hear the rustling of leaves on the trees, something he didn't remember ever pausing to listen to before. The world even smelled more alive. He took deep breaths, filled his lungs with the fresh, cool air.

He took Laci's body out of the pool and dragged it inside, where he dried it with towels.

Then he stepped into the bathroom, looked at his face in the mirror, and smiled a defiant, unrepentant smile.

He felt good, as though everything might work out, after all.

He felt utterly and intensely alive.

That night he would, no doubt, sleep like a baby. Perhaps he would dream a peculiar but strangely comforting dream—that he was an infant in Amber's arms, nursing at her breast as she walked along a pristine beach, magically growing a little in her arms with every wave that crashed, so that he was soon a child running along the shore with her, maturing with each step in the soft sand, slowly becoming a man, then suddenly taking her in his arms, kissing her, gently lowering her into the foam at water's edge and making love with her.

Chapter 23
STAYING ALIVE

When Modesto police officers John Evers, Matt Spurlock, and Sergeant Byron Duerfeldt visited Scott and Laci Peterson's home on Covena Avenue the next day, they found no hard evidence of foul play. The place was decked out for Christmas, with a glittering tree in one corner of the dining room, and presents piled high. The living room was nice and neat, furnished with overstuffed furniture. Leftover pizza was sitting in an open box on the kitchen counter. There was no evidence of a struggle.

Scott had been very nearly his perfect self in orchestrating what he hoped would be the perfect murder.

However, a few things did strike the officers as odd.

A bright blue bucket and two mops were leaning against an exterior wall outside the side door to the house. The bucket was wet, as was the sidewalk nearby. It looked as if someone had cleaned something up.

A throw rug near the back door was crumpled, as if something had been dragged over it.

Scott explained that when he had left to go fishing near the Berkeley Marina (before returning to find his wife missing), Laci had been doing some cleaning. When he had returned, he had found the mops in the bucket, still filled with water. So he had emptied it.

The cat and dog, he said, were probably responsible for the rug being out of place.

Before officers could intervene, he straightened out the rug.

Throughout the entire investigation, including extensive searches of the Peterson home, police would be unable to turn up a "smoking gun" to eventually present at his murder trial. There was a peculiar indentation roughly in the shape of a body in the comforter atop the Petersons' bed, but no blood-soaked mattress. There were no clumps of hair. Scott was never found to have Laci's skin under his fingernails, or scratches on his arms or face. There was no eyewitness. There had been no screaming heard coming from the house. There was no murder weapon.

For Scott, things had gone just about according to plan.

That was the good news, and the bad news. Because Scott's

plan was itself fatally flawed. It included three elements that would lead any decent detective to suspect Scott in the disappearance of his wife and unborn child.

- First, the idea that a man would go fishing on a cold morning before Christmas Eve, leaving his pregnant wife to clean house, was tough for anyone to believe. It would direct police to search Scott's boat and his storage facility, finding not only one of Laci's hairs on a pair of Scott's pliers but residue from the cement Scott had used for his homemade anchors.

- Second, Scott told police he had been fishing in the San Francisco Bay when he knew he had just dumped his wife and unborn son's bodies there. That would ultimately put him at the scene of the crime when their remains turned up. Indeed, Jackie Peterson would later protest to her son: "I can't imagine anyone being stupid enough to say they went fishing in the Berkeley Bay after having committed a crime there. I mean, not even you, Scott."

- Third, the fact that Scott had failed to do much to hide his affair with Amber from anyone, or at least pretend it was over, would inevitably prove his marriage was less than the "perfect" one he initially described.

There is one central reason why Scott failed to plan more completely and put forward a convincing alibi: he lacked intuition, so he assumed others lacked it, too, including Laci's family and the police. He placed no real value on the truth and could not resonate with it, so he could not know which elements of his story would strike others as patently false.

He would have made a lousy detective.

And he made a lousy criminal.

Scott Peterson's lies, after all, had been found out by the women in his life more than once.

Laci had met his girlfriend Janet when Janet walked in on Laci and Scott in bed. Apparently, Scott hadn't even gone to the trouble of making sure that Janet believed he was out of town, on a vacation, when Laci came to visit his apartment that weekend.

Laci hadn't missed the fact that Scott was using her to make Lauren Putnat jealous by seating her in Lauren's waitressing section of the Pacific Café. Laci ended up hysterical in the rest room.

Lauren, of couse, knew exactly what Scott was up to.

And it is hard to believe Laci would not have noticed anything odd about Katy Hansen's reaction to her kissing Scott and placing a lei around his neck at his college graduation. Scott hadn't even been concerned enough to play sick that day or to tell Katy that Laci was an old girlfriend who insisted on being there to wish him well.

It had only taken Shawn Sibley a couple of days to figure out that Scott had lied to her and Amber about never having been married.

Scott wasn't even a very good salesman for Tradecorp. And that was no surprise. He would not have been able to sense exactly what would *move* a buyer to agree to purchase something from him. He might make wildly exaggerated claims about the products he was representing, but they would *seem* exaggerated to potential buyers.

Scott Peterson could lie with ease and without remorse or shame, but, having insulated himself from all real emotion as a child, having built thicker and thicker walls around his soul, he lacked the sensitivity to lie well.

All the chapters of his life story, including his alibi, read like fiction.

Chapter 24
THE STRANGER

If the story Scott Peterson had to tell wasn't very convincing, the storyteller was even less so. As a person imitating a person, a mimicker, he was out of his element. He had nothing to work with.

The detectives, including Al Brocchini, a seventeen-year police-force veteran assigned to the Peterson case, weren't anything like the women who had hung on Scott's every word. Scott couldn't mirror their likes and dislikes and listen so intently to them that they would be seduced into believing his innocence. They really didn't care that he was good-looking and had a nice smile. They weren't predisposed to believing him, hoping he was for real and would marry them. They wouldn't care if he was a vegetarian just like them, or a pet lover just like them, or whether he was religious just like them.

Now it was all about Scott. He wasn't anyone's understudy anymore. Lee and Jackie couldn't give him a down payment on his innocence or buy him a Get Out of Jail Free card. There was nowhere to hide.

From the very beginning, he looked like a deer caught in headlights.

He was stiff, inhuman.

He was like Mersault in Camus's *The Stranger*, arrested for the murder of his mother, speaking for the first time with his lawyer:

The investigators had learned that I had "shown insensitivity" the day of Maman's [his mother's] funeral. "You understand," my lawyer said, "it's a little embarrassing for me to have to ask you this. But it's very important. And it will be a strong argument for the prosecution if I can't come up with some answers." He wanted me to help him. He asked if I had felt any sadness that day. The question caught me by surprise and it seemed to me that I would have been very embarrassed if I'd had to ask it. Nevertheless I answered that I had pretty much lost the habit of analyzing myself and that it was hard for me to tell him what he wanted to know. I probably did love Maman, but that didn't change anything. At one time or another all normal people have wished their loved ones dead. Here the lawyer interrupted me and he seemed very upset.

When Scott had first called to tell Sharon Rocha that he couldn't find Laci, he described her as "missing." But he didn't sound panicked.

Later that day, Detective Brocchini visited the Peterson home and began looking inside Scott's truck, which was parked close to Laci's Land Rover. When he opened Scott's driver's side door it bumped into the side of the Rover.

"I can move the truck forward," Scott offered. He took out a glove and suggested he hold it in place to protect against a ding.

Brocchini rightly wondered why a man whose wife was missing would be so worried about whether one of his vehicles might end up scratched. Wasn't it more important to make sure every potential clue be identified that could result in Laci being found?

Days later, Scott would interrupt a police officer who was making a list of items he was taking for evidence from the Peterson home. He wanted to slip some pieces of paper under the one the police officer was writing on, so he wouldn't scratch the table.

The trouble for Scott was that he wasn't acting anymore, or didn't know exactly how to pull off this role. He really did care more about whether his truck or Laci's Rover or the dining room table got damaged than he did about collecting clues. After all, Laci was already dead. Why ruin a car or a nice piece of furniture over nothing?

A little later, as the search continued, Scott walked over to Sharon Rocha, who was on the front lawn watching. "You know," he told her, "if they find blood anywhere that doesn't mean anything. I'm a sportsman. Just look at my hands. I could drop blood anywhere."

Why did he already seem focused on establishing his innocence? Rocha might have wondered.

The answer was simple: that *was* his focus, because he was guilty and didn't want to get caught.

Whereas romance freed Scott to be someone other than himself, to fabricate convincing tales on the fly, it seemed that killing deprived him of his mask. Now he looked pretty much like what he was: a murderer.

The only thing still hidden from view was the fact that he had been murdered himself, suffocated as a child, essentially held underwater until he agreed to stop breathing.

After Detective Brocchini and Officer Evers searched the warehouse where Scott stored his new boat, taking photographs and noting the concrete debris inside the boat's rib line, they asked Scott back to Modesto police headquarters. He agreed to go.

But before the three men left, Scott told Brocchini he hoped he wouldn't show any of the photos to his boss, since Tradecorp owned the warehouse and might frown on him using it for personal items.

Again, Brocchini noted that Scott seemed more concerned about keeping his good name with his employer than finding his wife.

And that was true. He was going to need a paycheck to keep romancing Amber Frey.

The three men sat down at headquarters. Scott agreed to provide a tape-recorded statement. In the middle of his interview, his cell phone rang. He answered it. It was Amy, Laci's younger half sister. He talked to her a bit and learned that several family members had congregated at his house, but he never inquired about how the search for Laci was going.

He didn't care.

He remained unemotional during questioning into the early morning hours.

He wasn't feeling much emotion.

He was forgetting or finding it impossible to act. What he really needed was a pretty, single female police officer who could cue him. "You must be feeling just awful, Scott," she could say.

"You have no idea," he could respond, welling up.

"Just tell me . . . I mean, you seem like such a good guy. Did you have anything to do with this?"

And he could have looked deeply into her eyes, let a tear or two go, shaken his head incredulously, and said, "You're kidding, right? You *know* I would never hurt anyone. You *know* who I am."

"I want to believe that. I really do."

"You can believe it. I would never lie to you. Ever. You can trust me."

Al Brocchini and John Evers didn't even have nice smiles for him.

Scott did make one meager attempt to connect with the officers on a human level, to appear distraught. But even his method of faking his pain seemed to point to his very real guilt.

According to Catherine Crier, in her book *A Deadly Game*, Scott inquired of Brocchini, "The only question I have . . . what about resources available? You saw my mother-in-law tonight, um, anyway, you saw some of my friends, myself. . . ."

"What do you mean?" Brocchini asked him.

"Counseling and that kind of thing. Can you give us the numbers or do I have to search . . ."

"No, I can give you those numbers. I just don't know. You're probably not going to get any answers today. It's Christmas, I mean."

"Yeah, of course. And there is no need to call if we find Laci in the next days."

"Yeah, I agree. I'll give you those numbers."

"I will need them."

Crier writes:

The question is chillingly obvious: How was Scott so sure that he would need counseling, only hours after Laci disappeared? Families of missing people are generally so caught up in the moment—and clinging so dearly to hope—that it's some time before counseling comes into play. Often the investigation and trial in a murder case so focuses the family that it's not until well after the verdict that members really acknowledge their grief and turn to counselors. Yet Scott was already sure he'd need that kind of assistance only hours into the search.

The reason Scott seemed certain what he and his family would need, of course, was that he was guessing at what people feel. He thought that mentioning counseling would imply that he understood his relatives were in pain, and that he was, too. The "subtly constructed reflex machine" was failing.

Soon everyone would see.

Chapter 25
SEARCHING

Scott Peterson kept a low profile in the first days after Laci's disappearance.

The Rocha family and their friends set up a command center at the local Red Lion Hotel and put together a $100,000 reward for information leading to Laci's safe return. Sharon Rocha, her husband, Ron Grantski, and Jackie and Lee Peterson appeared on the news and gave press conferences every chance they could, getting the word out that Laci was missing.

Hundreds of volunteers searched the Modesto area and distributed flyers with Laci's picture on them.

Scott avoided almost all of that. He explained to reporters that if he granted interviews it would take the focus off Laci, and put it on him.

That statement was probably true, though not in the way Scott intended it. If viewers were able to look at and listen to him for long enough, they would probably get the idea Laci was already dead, and that he had killed her.

But I believe there was another reason Scott shied away from the media: he didn't want Amber Frey to see him on television or catch his photograph in a newspaper. He was actually hoping that he could make it through the entire investigation into Laci's murder without ever being charged by the police or found out by his girlfriend. He was desperate to continue his relationship with her.

Amber Frey was no Janet Ilse or Katy Hansen to Scott Peterson. She wasn't like any of the other women Scott had probably romanced since marrying Laci. She was the one he had to have, had to keep.

Whether it was timing or chemistry or both, Amber was part of the perfect psychological storm that had started December 20, 1945, swept through the decades, and caused the sea to swell as Scott launched his boat holding Laci and Conner's bodies from the Berkeley Marina on December 24. She was the one he convinced himself he was willing to kill for and willing to be reborn for.

Scott was shying away from more than publicity, though. To

police, he seemed uninterested in the progress of the investigation. He wasn't calling for updates. He wasn't pressing them to work harder or faster or to bring more officers onto the case or to recruit outside resources.

Detective Brocchini, on the other hand, was after him to take a polygraph.

He hadn't agreed to it yet. And soon his family would hire attorney Kirk McAllister, who would advise him not to take it.

It is very possible, of course, that McAllister had Scott take a polygraph in his office. Many criminal defense attorneys own their own polygraph machines. It is not unusual for me to get a call from an attorney asking me to evaluate his or her client for a possibly insanity plea and hear, "Just between you and me, Keith, he's still saying he didn't do it. But the polygraph is a mess."

Chances are, Scott Peterson's polygraph was a mess, too. Otherwise, you can be sure the results would have been leaked to the media.

On December 26, Scott spoke with Amber Frey. She had no idea that a search was under way in Modesto for Scott's pregnant wife.

Scott had sent Frey's daughter, Ayiana, a sky-gazer toy that projected stars onto the walls and ceiling. Enclosed was a note that said, "To my girls . . . The angels are watching over you. Where's the first star in the sky?"

The two talked the next day, too. Scott said he was in New York, en route to Paris. When Amber worried aloud whether he was being faithful to her, he assured her he was. He told her the two of them had a future together and apologized for spending so much time traveling. "Next year," he said, "will be different. You and I will be spending a lot of holidays together."

When Scott called Amber back at 7:00 P.M. they had a bad connection. He told her he was boarding his flight. He had to run.

"Something was wrong here," Amber Frey writes in her book, *Witness*. "Feminine intuition had been telling me that I should watch my step with Scott Peterson, but I'd been so in love with the idea of him—of this perfect man, of our perfect romance—that I refused to hear it."

The next day Amber went to church and prayed for clarity about her relationship with Scott.

Scott tried her twice by phone that night, and she called him back, but the two never connected.

On December 29, the next day, Amber's friend Richard Byrd, himself a police officer, phoned and gave her what she had prayed for: Scott Peterson lived in Modesto; his wife was missing.

Amber couldn't believe what she was hearing. She asked Byrd to check to make absolutely sure he was talking about the same Scott Peterson she had been dating. *Her* Scott Peterson.

At 1:40 A.M. on December 30, Byrd called her back with the bad news.

At 1:43 A.M., Amber called the Modesto police. She agreed to be interviewed at her home at 11:00 A.M.

Al Brocchini and another detective named Jon Buehler arrived promptly at her door. Amber told them everything she knew about Scott Peterson. She also agreed to tape all her future phone calls with him.

Scott would never admit to killing his wife on any of those calls and would never waver in his assertions that he wanted a future with Amber.

Amber writes in *Witness:*

> . . . Clearly Scott wanted me to believe that we had a solid future. Even then, on the phone, with Laci missing and hundreds of people searching for her, he took the time to tell me that our relationship was very beautiful, and that it would evolve over time. "You know, in my mind, we could be wonderful together," he said. "I could care for you in any and every way."

There was just one little problem with Scott's plans. The police weren't just listening in, they were closing in.

On New Year's Eve, as more than a thousand people held a candlelight vigil for Laci, Scott was careful to stay away from the cameras. He avoided joining his family and Laci's when they stood on the podium and spoke to the crowd.

At midnight, he called Amber. They talked for seventy minutes. He told her he wanted to be with her and raise Ayiana with her. He said he felt the two of them could "fulfill each other . . . forever."

But the most interesting exchange occurred when Amber brought up a book that Scott had been reading. "What book was that?" she asked him.

"Jack Kerouac," Scott said. "It was, unm . . . hitchhiking across the country . . . oh, shoot, what's his book? Late sixties movie . . . I can't think of the name right now." [*On the Road*]

"That's okay. Good book, though? Did you enjoy it?"

"Yeah, it was interesting 'cause it's a . . . it was interesting because I never had a prolonged period of freedom like that from responsibility, you know. . . ."

A little of Scott's truth was leaking out again, even if it was an understatement. Because from the day Jackie Peterson brought him home from the hospital, he had never known an hour of freedom, never mind a "prolonged period" of it.

Chapter 26
I THINK I KNOW

By January 2, the police were publicly asking for help verifying Scott's alibi while privately continuing to tape his calls with Amber Frey. They had not gone public with the fact that Scott and Amber had been lovers.

Scott starting asking Amber about whether she'd seen various innocuous items in the newspaper, trying to determine whether she was likely to find out that he wasn't really jetting around the globe, that he was struggling to keep his head above water as police closed in on him.

Amber didn't let on that she knew about his deception.

On January 4, he stepped out again from behind his mask of sanity and told her a little bit about his truth. During a phone conversation that meandered through several topics he brought up movies he liked. "The best movie ever made," he said, "is *The Shining*." He said it scared "the hell out of him."

In *The Shining*, of course, Jack Nicholson plays a crazed man trying to kill his wife and son.

He told her that "the only thing keeping me grounded are my hands on your waist."

It may well have felt that way to him. Amber was the only one who he thought still saw him the way he wanted to be seen. And more than ever, she represented freedom and love to him, when almost everyone else was wondering whether he was a murderer.

Things got worse for Scott on January 5. *People* magazine had published an article about Laci, along with a photograph of Scott. And on a phone call with Amber, she told him that a friend of hers had called and left her an urgent message.

"Sauki called," Amber said, "and left me a message and said she was worried about me. She was in between flights and she said she needed to talk to me when she got back into town, and I have no idea."

"Huh? Weird," Scott said. "She left like a cryptic message?"

". . . I'm scared," Amber said. "I have no idea what she's talking about."

Even that ominous call didn't make Scott cut off communication with Amber. He needed her. He called her the next day and confessed that he had been lying to her. He wasn't traveling in Europe at all. He was at home in Modesto.

"The girl I'm married to, her name is Laci," he said. "She disappeared just before Christmas. . . . For the past two weeks, I've been in Modesto with her family and mine searching for her. She just disappeared, and no one knows where she's been. I can't tell you more because I need you to be protected from the media. . . ."

But he did tell her more. "The media has been telling everyone that I had something to do with her disappearance. So, the past two weeks, I've been hunted by the media. And I just . . . I don't want you to be involved in this, to protect yourself. I know that I've, you know, I've destroyed. And I, God, I hope . . . I hope so much that . . . this doesn't hurt you."

"How could it not affect me?" Amber asked.

"It does. And I just—"

"How . . . how . . . could you possibly think this would not affect me?"

"Amber," Scott said. "I know it does."

But he didn't. As a dead man, a person imitating a person, he lacked even that much empathy. He couldn't imagine what Amber had felt when her friend Richard Byrd had told her the awful truth about *her* Scott Peterson.

Later in the conversation, Amber asked Scott, "Why would you tell me this on December ninth? [Why would you tell me] that you have lost your wife and I'm sorry I can't tell until after I get back from Europe and about this tragedy, and I asked you are you ready for me? Oh, absolutely. This will be the first holidays without my wife. I'm going to spend them with my family in Maine. Is this not what you said?"

"It is," Scott answered.

"It is?"

"—and I . . . It is, and I . . . it is."

"And how do you explain all of a sudden you tell me it's a national search?"

"It is, yes," Scott said.

"How is that just not such a coincidence?" Amber asked.

"If you think I had something to do with her disappearance," Scott said, ". . . er, that is so wrong."

"Really?"

"Yes, it is."

Still later, Amber tried to get Scott to clarify the strategy he had had in mind to keep her. "Okay, how . . . now again, you were assuming we would stay together and you tell me all these future things with me," Amber said. "How would you explain a newborn child of yours, that I mean I would assume she would want you to have regular visits with this child . . . right?"

"Sweetie," Scott responded, "I'm so sorry, but I can't tell you—"

"Why can't you?" Amber asked.

"—about those things right now."

"Why? Why? Why not right now?"

"It would hurt entirely too many people."

"Now is this child yours?"

"Sweetie . . . I'm sorry I keep saying that [Amber had asked him to stop calling her Sweetie], you asked me not to. Amber, I cannot tell you."

"Is this child yours?" she persisted.

"I can't tell you these things right now."

"Why?"

"The only . . ." Scott stammered, ". . . the only things I just I needed you to know and I hope that . . . I hope that . . . you are not . . . you know . . . God, I . . . I . . . I think I know I hurt you."

A little more of Scott Peterson's truth had leaked out from behind his mask of sanity. Having lied to Amber Frey about being married, having spent time with her precious twenty-month-old daughter, Ayiana, having told her he was duck hunting in Maine and on business in Europe while he was actually killing his wife and unborn son and faking a meager interest in the search for them, he had the sneaking suspicion he might have hurt her.

I think I know I hurt you. It was a report from the emotional no-man's-land where Scott Peterson had lived his entire life, having cut himself off from his own pain, leaving him devoid of empathy, guessing at the emotions of others.

Before the phone conversation with Amber was over, she had essentially accused him of killing Laci, calling her disappearance "the biggest coincidence ever."

Scott insisted he wasn't "evil like that," then broke down into tears.

"Save your tears," Amber bristled. "I did everything possible to protect my baby and me. I told you this. I worked forty-plus hours a week—because I wasn't going to ask for help from anyone. And I did this on my own. I went to school. I had my baby. I did this all with her. I didn't need this in my life. I didn't need for someone to come in and to fuck all of it up."

"I know that, Amber," he said, crying.

That, he knew. He didn't *think* he knew. He knew.

Maybe that's why Scott Peterson had kept Amber Frey in his life, and still seemed to want to. Maybe she could get through to him—to the *real* Scott Peterson, the one he hardly remembered himself, the one imprisoned behind walls he had built to keep out his mother and father, that he never stopped building, that eventually kept out the whole world, leaving him forgotten, left for dead.

Maybe, even as Amber was collecting evidence that would help condemn him to death, she made Scott feel alive.

Chapter 27
HIDEOUT

During the second week of January, Scott Peterson arranged to stay with his half sister, Anne Bird, at her home in Berkeley.

He was leaking the truth everywhere now, even in the view he chose. Anne's house overlooked the San Francisco Bay.

After thanking Anne and her husband, Tim, for putting him up, he said, "You can't believe what it's like down there [in Modesto]. I'm basically a prisoner of my own face."

A prisoner of my own face. He had that right. Scott was locked behind the mask of sanity he had worn for three decades. And, at some unconscious level, he knew it.

While he seemed exhausted when he arrived, he drank a fair bit of wine with dinner the first night in Berkeley and became very animated—as though, according to Anne, he "didn't have a care in the world."

Two days later, Anne saw him flirt with her baby-sitter, a young, pretty woman who had the same effect on him as the wine. He became energized.

Alcohol and sex, Scott Peterson's drugs, still worked for him. They still helped him get an edge over reality, some distance on the truth.

But the truth always wins.

On January 15, the police told Sharon Rocha and Ron Grantski that Scott had been having an affair prior to Laci's disappearance. They also revealed that he had recently taken out a $250,000 insurance policy on her.

Sharon Rocha dissolved into tears. "Why did he have to kill her?" she asked Detectives Al Brocchini and Jon Buehler. It took her a very long time for her to regain her composure.

Meanwhile, Detectives Craig Grogan and Phil Owen were breaking the news to Lee and Jackie Peterson.

After being shown photographs of Amber and Scott together, Lee had a few questions. He wanted to know how old the photographs were. When he was told they were taken around Christmas, he wanted to know how the police had obtained them. Then he wanted to know specifically whether Amber had turned them over voluntarily.

Lee was thinking more like a defense attorney than the father of a man who had been secretly romancing another woman while his pregnant wife was missing. He was trying to keep the walls around Scott's truth from crumbling.

But then Lee asked a question that let a little of his own truth out. "[Does] she know him as someone else?" he asked.

Either Lee knew that Scott was in the habit of concealing his real identity in order to seduce women, or he was projecting— harking back to his own episode of using a different name, when he had run away from financial problems (or raced away in his Ferrari).

Grogan told the Petersons how Scott had met Amber through Shawn Sibley and that he had lied to her, telling her he was un- married. He also told them that Scott was still in touch with Am- ber by phone.

"I'm shocked," Lee said.

Then Detective Owen said more about how the pictures were obtained. "She was under the impression that her and Scott had a relationship and she was proud of him," he said, "so she was sending out Christmas cards to her friends. She came to us with the pictures."

"She came to you?" Lee asked. He was incredulous. "Since Laci's disappearance? Why in the hell would she do that?"

Lee literally couldn't figure it out. Why would a woman who had been lied to and manipulated, who thought that her boyfriend might be involved in the disappearance of his preg- nant wife bother going to police? What was in it for her?

Lee had tipped his hand. It sounded as though his moral foundation might be a little shaky. But maybe he didn't think anyone was really listening. Maybe he was used to dealing with the dead guys around the fake card table at home, throwing back imaginary shots of scotch in antique glasses.

Days later, when Jackie didn't know anyone was listening, she left this voice mail on Scott's phone, which had been tapped by police:

> I wanted to talk to you about something. I would [think] that you should deny, deny, deny. I was told that years ago by an attorney, and I think you should talk to Kirk and do that. . . . I had to do that at the time. I'm sorry,

but that's what I had to do and I really feel that that's right. Um, that you must deny these things, not to the press, not to anybody, but to your family. Because . . . it will be talked about and it could leak and it's not good if there is any truth to your [unintelligible]. I'm not saying there is. . . .

Chapter 28
A REAL MOTHER'S GRIEF AND RAGE

On January 16, the *National Enquirer* published an article detailing Scott Peterson's affair with Amber Frey. While withholding her name, the newspaper printed photographs of them together.

Sharon Rocha called Scott from home. Police recorded the conversation.

Scott answered.

"Where are you?" Sharon asked. She didn't give Scott the chance to answer. "Well, since you've managed to lose all of my confidence in you, what I want to know is, where is my daughter at, Scott?"

"I wish I knew, Mom," he said. "I wish I knew where she is."

Sharon was livid. "You do know," she shot back. "You do know where she is and I want you to tell me. Where is Laci and her baby? Where did you put them?"

"Where is my wife and our child? I don't know."

"You killed my daughter, didn't you?"

"No, I didn't, Mom," Scott said.

Mom. Not a good sign.

If Amber Frey had the greatest chance of getting Scott to take off his mask, Sharon Rocha had the least. She was his wife's *mother*, worthy of contempt, complicit in his destruction. In his mind, he owed her nothing.

"Yes, you did, Scott," Sharon said. "And I want to know, just let me bring my daughter home, okay? That's all I want. I don't want anything else from you. I want you to tell me where my daughter is. I want to bury my daughter. Now would you tell me where she is, Scott?"

Those words are enough to bring tears to my eyes, and it is not my first time reading them. I can't help thinking what it would be like for my wife to have to make a call like the one Sharon Rocha was making. I can't help *empathizing* with Sharon, feeling a tiny, tiny percentage of what she must have felt.

Scott Peterson felt nothing more than a spectator's interest in his mother-in-law's grief and rage, a kind of detached curiosity about why she was so upset.

He may even have been surprised at how angry she seemed.

Sharon's plea to let her bury her daughter would certainly fall on deaf ears. Scott didn't like the whole idea of a mother burying her child, anyway. He'd been buried alive by his a long time ago. "Don't know where she is," he told her. "I want my wife. . . ."

"Stop lying," Sharon broke in. "I'm tired of your lies. You have looked me in the eye . . . for weeks and been lying to me. You have looked me in the eye for years and been lying to me. Now where is she?"

"I wish I knew."

He did wish that. He wished Laci was deep in the Bay, never to be found.

"You do know. Stop lying," Sharon begged. "For once in your life take some responsibility and tell the goddamn truth. Where is my daughter?"

"I want her home, Mom and—"

Mom.

"Shut up," Sharon insisted. "Don't tell me such stupid things. You tell me where she is. Where did you put her? Scott, tell me where she is."

"I'm sorry—"

"And you can run away . . . you can go do whatever the fuck you want, but tell me where my daughter is."

"I'm sorry."

"I have every right to know where you put Laci."

"We all have a right to know where Laci is . . ." Scott said evenly.

"Quit lying to me," Sharon screamed. "Don't bullshit me. You tell me where she is."

Scott spoke in a monotone: "We all want her home."

"Shut up," Sharon demanded. "You are such a fucking liar. You make me sick, Scott. Where is Laci? I want to be able to bury my daughter. Now tell me what you did with her."

What sense would it make to tell her? Scott might have been thinking. To him, Sharon sounded insane for even asking. First of all, telling her would get him put in jail. Secondly, if he was lucky, there was nothing left of her to bury, anyway. The fish would see to that. "I want her and our child home . . ." he said calmly.

"Oh, shut up. You're disgusting. Do you know there's not a person in this town who wants to see your face? Now you tell me where she is and then you can get the hell out of here. Tell me where she is. I want my daughter, Scott. That's all I want from you. I don't care what happens to you."

"Mom, we all want her back," he said. Translation: *Mom*, you can talk until you are as blue in the face as your daughter, and I will not be moved by your suffering.

If Sharon Rocha had any doubt in her mind whether Scott Peterson had murdered her daughter, she could have erased it by listening to the tape police were making of her conversation with him. Never did her accusation that he had killed Laci cause him any anger. Never was he incredulous. He was inhuman in his responses and dead even in his tone of voice. She got nothing back from him. She might as well have been talking to herself.

For the first time since she had met him, Scott Peterson wasn't pretending. He was letting her know exactly who he was.

Chapter 29
GOOD MORNING AMERICA

Once word was out that Scott Peterson had been having an affair with Amber Frey, he stopped paying lip service to fears that he might overshadow his missing wife by talking to reporters. He began to do high-profile interviews, including one with *Good Morning America* co-host Diane Sawyer. On January 28, 2003 he sat down for an interview with her.

I commented on that interview on *The Oprah Winfrey Show*. What follows is my more complete analysis.

Scott was anything but camera ready. He was handicapped again by his own lack of intuition. He couldn't understand the degree to which people—including Sawyer—might be able to *sense* his guilt. If avoiding prosecution and conviction for the murders of Laci and Conner were his goals, he would have been better off staying home.

The error in judgment he made stepping into the media spotlight wasn't because, as some would later theorize, he thought he was smarter than everyone else, it was because he thought he was *just like* everyone else. He thought his mask of sanity was more perfect than it really was.

"I think everybody sitting at home wants the answer to the same question," Sawyer began. "Did you murder your wife?"

"No, no I did not," Scott answered, "and I had absolutely nothing to do with her disappearance. And you use the word 'murder' and, yeah, I mean that is a possibility. Um . . . it's not one we're ready to accept and it creeps in my mind late at night and early in the morning. And during the day all we can think about is the right resolution—is to find her well."

"But as you know," Sawyer said, "increasingly in the public, suspicion has turned on you."

"Yes, definitely."

"Did you ever hit her? Did you ever injure her?"

Scott was about to stumble: "No, no, my God, no," he said. "Um, violence towards women is—is unapproachable. It is the most disgusting act to me."

He went on from there, but he had already lost sympathy with viewers, even if they would not have been able to say just why. It was his lack of real feeling. Asked whether he had struck his wife, he hadn't reacted with disgust, saying, "That's ridiculous, Diane. People have a hell of a nerve saying these things when someone might have killed my wife, and I'm out there trying to find her. Check any ER you want to looking for Laci getting help for domestic violence. Get every police report you can. I never, ever struck my wife. I loved her. It sickens me to hear you suggest otherwise."

Instead, Scott had retreated to a statement that was highly impersonal. It sounded like a lifeless cliché: "Um, violence towards women is—is unapproachable."

It was the very best he could do.

"Amber Frey came forward . . ." Sawyer prompted him.

"I'm glad she did," Scott said.

"You are?"

"Definitely."

"Why?"

"It's the appropriate thing to do. It really shows what a person of character she is. Um . . . and it allows us to . . . um . . . get back to looking for Laci."

Again, Scott sounded mechanical and not believable. An honest person would hardly maintain it was a good thing to have your mistress go public after your pregnant wife has gone missing. And even if someone actually *felt* what Scott was describing, it might come out sounding more human: "Sure, I'm glad she came forward. I felt incredibly guilty about seeing her and hiding it from my in-laws, especially with what's happened. I feel better that it's out in the open. I can at least deal with it now, answer everybody's questions and get it out of the way. It's a lousy thing I did, but it's a distraction at the moment. I want my wife and child back."

"Did your wife find out about it?" Sawyer asked him.

"I told my wife."

"When?"

"In um . . . early December."

"Did it cause a rupture in the marriage?"

Again, Scott's response lacked any authenticity. He couldn't access enough internal emotion to fashion a convincing lie. He was a much better mimic than he was an actor. "It was not . . .

um . . . a positive, obviously. It's a . . . you know, inappropriate, um, but it was not something we weren't . . . um . . . dealing with.

"A lot of arguing?" Sawyer inquired.

"No, no, you know I can't say that—that even, you know, she was okay with the idea. But it wasn't anything that would break us apart."

"There wasn't a lot of anger."

"No."

It was not a positive, obviously. Not a positive? Scott's use of language sounded mechanical, like a computer trying to imitate a man. That was, of course, approximately what was unfolding on camera—the taping of a "subtly constructed reflex machine" of the kind Hervey Cleckley had written about in *The Mask of Sanity*.

A normal man, lying convincingly, might have responded this way to Sawyer's questions about marital discord: "C'mon, you have to know the answer to that question, Diane. She was pissed, right? Wouldn't *you* be? I mean, for God's sake, she was pregnant. I did a really bad thing, and she let me know it. Laci was no pushover. She didn't leave me that day, but she might have a month later, or two months. These things *work* on people. I know that. We both know that. But, again, c'mon . . . This is all bullshit. I had an affair. I didn't kidnap my wife or kill her. This is ridiculous. We have to find Laci. Every minute we talk about Amber is just about selling newspapers. It's a waste."

Sawyer later asked, "Tell me about the state of your marriage. What . . . What kind of marriage was it?"

"God, I mean the first word that comes to mind," Scott answered, "is . . . you know . . . glorious. I mean we took care of each other very well. Um . . . she was amazing—is amazing."

Scott was having a little problem with his tenses. He sounded as if he were certain his wife was already dead, that she *was* amazing—before she was murdered.

Toward the end of the interview segment, Sawyer noted, "You haven't mentioned your son."

"Hmmm . . . that was . . . it's so hard."

Scott had stumbled again, mixing up his tenses. Because the

truth was that he was already over killing Conner. Past tense. It *was* hard for him—for about three minutes. Maybe.

"Tell me about the nursery," Sawyer went on.

"I can't go in there," Scott said. "That door is closed until there's someone to put in there. But it's ready."

Someone to put in there. Again, Scott's response sounded mechanical and impersonal. *Someone?* Sawyer could have asked. *Just anyone? Aren't we talking about* your son *here?*

A real person might have said, "That door is closed until Laci is found, hopefully alive, hopefully able to bring my son into the world, so we can take him home and keep him safe in his room. I won't touch a thing in there until I know they're either okay or they're dead. And I just have to keep believing they're okay, even though it's hard after a month. It's beyond anything I've ever dealt with. You can't possibly know how hard it is unless you've lived through something like this yourself. And I pray you never have to."

Sawyer kept up the pressure. "Are you afraid the police will arrest you?" she asked Scott.

"No. I know there is—there's no basis. I mean I had nothing to do with her disappearance. So there is no possible evidence or anything like that."

Where was Scott's fear? Where was his rage? *There's no basis. There is no possible evidence.* He sounded like an arms dealer lying to Congress. The audience was looking for something real, something genuine, something human. They weren't hearing it or seeing it.

A real person would have said something like: "Am I afraid? Of course. I'm terrified. I mean, they're focusing on me as a suspect. I can't believe this is happening to me. I feel like I'm locked in some third-rate thriller. I loved my wife. I would never hurt my wife. And if they think I might have killed her—which is utterly insane—what's to stop them from trumping up some crazy case against me? The cops are lazy. There are leads they need to follow that they aren't following. I'm here to tell you what they are."

But there were no credible and substantial leads the police had failed to pursue.

"Have they given you reason to think this, that you're their prime suspect?" Sawyer asked.

"Um . . . yeah, I mean with, you know, the whole, you know,

search warrants for the cars and things like that, certainly. Um, you know, a search warrant for the home . . . um . . . and to get specific to a car obviously they're—they're looking at, you know, me."

A search warrant for *the home*. Scott was messing up, yet again. Why couldn't he even bear to call it *our home*?

Here's what viewers didn't hear: "Of course they're focusing on me, Diane. I was having an affair when she disappeared. It's always the husband, right? Well, not this time. This time they're screwing up. This time, they're wasting precious days thinking about me when I wouldn't hurt a fly. God! I can't believe this is happening! I mean, imagine how crazy this is. I screw around on my wife, okay. Fine. But I don't *kill* women. I mean, Jesus! Give me a break."

There was something else that viewers didn't hear during the interview. It would have been the ultimate gauntlet thrown down to all the idiotic detectives bothering Scott when he was innocent.

"I'm willing to take a polygraph test right on this show, Diane," he could have said. "Get a certified expert, give me ten tests, and we'll have each one analyzed. I know these things aren't admissible in court, but I don't care. I have nothing to hide. If they're even good eighty percent of the time, I'll come up clean eight of the ten times we try it. So let's go. When do I come back on?"

That wasn't going to happen.

Several hours after the interview was over, Scott called his parents' house. Jackie answered. Police were recording the call. The exchange was quoted in, and inspired the title of, Catherine Crier's book, *A Deadly Game*.

Scott told Jackie that his attorney, Kirk McAllister, had met with the DA, who had proposed a deal: " 'If Scott tells us where the body is, we won't kill him.' "

> "Oh, my God," Jackie said.
> "Yeah, the DA thinks I'm guilty, too," Scott said.
> Lee Peterson picked up. "What are you saying about the DA?"
> "Oh, he made me an offer. If I tell him where the body is, they won't put me to death."
> "Oh jeesh," Lee said.

"He [Kirk] just said they're just struggling to find anything, you know that's why they call me and all that weird stuff they've done, like go down and meet with you. They call me and say, 'We're searching the bay again, Scott.' They're trying to, you know, crack people. He [Kirk] said that if they had the stuff that they say they have, I would be locked up right now."

"Kirk is pretty confident you're in good shape, though?"

"Yeah," Scott said, "I mean, Kirk tells me I'm playing a deadly game here. But he is pretty confident."

"Kirk says you're playing a deadly game?" Jackie Peterson repeated.

"Yup."

"Jeez." Jackie sighed.

". . . Kirk knows if the DA thinks they have enough to arrest me and they arrest me, there's no bail, it's a capital case," Scott went on.

"Can you handle that with no bail?" Jackie asked.

"God," Scott said, "I can't imagine being in prison, you know, for who knows how long. . . . But they have to have something credible to go on. They won't and they can't, so I'm not really worried about it."

"I don't think they have anything, they couldn't have," Lee Peterson said.

"No, there's nothing to have," Scott said.

"No, that's what I mean," Lee said.

Jeesh. Jeez. Golly. It's hard to keep in mind the fact that these are parents discussing the potential execution of their son. No one is crying. No one is pleading for an end to all the insanity, the living hell of being an innocent man facing lethal injection. No one is offering even a modicum of emotional support to anyone else.

Because Scott Peterson was already dead. And he was talking to the people who had killed him. He couldn't really expect a lot of comfort.

The next day, Scott was interviewed by journalist Gloria Gomez for KOVR Channel 13 in Sacramento. He had the same

problem with platitudes and inhuman responses to highly emotional questions. He was unshakable, forgiving, patient, kind—at
a moment when his wife and unborn child were missing, when
his in-laws thought he was to blame, and when police considered him the lead suspect.

Two excerpts should suffice:

Gomez: How do you feel though, that you know the
Ro . . . the Rocha family says they can't trust you?

Peterson: They're, they're wonderful people, the Rocha
family. I know that you know we all have love between us
and I know that we will all keep searching for Laci. . . .

"But, Scott, how do you *feel* about being branded a killer by
your in-laws?" Gomez could have followed up. "Aren't you angry? And how can you say they love you, if they think you killed
their daughter?"

Scott's responses lacked emotional authenticity, because he
was not an authentic human being. He was a person imitating a
person.

The interview was almost over when Scott told viewers exactly how he felt about his pregnant wife:

Gomez: Okay, I just want to ask you one last thing if
that's okay. Um, about Laci, because I know you really
get choked up when you talk about it. Tell me what you
love about Laci.

Peterson: God, what . . . you know . . . I think you can
sum it up pretty easily with looking at her photograph.
The photograph of her big smile in the press.

Here's the problem. If you could sum up your love for another person by looking at that person's smile in a photograph,
then there would be a lot of people buying frames in Hallmark
stores and becoming attached to the smiling people on the pho-
tocopied paper inside them.

All Scott knew about Laci Peterson was what was on the surface. Her smile. That she was female. That she watched Martha Stewart.

A decent video camera would record the same observations.

The truth was Scott Peterson never loved Laci. He never even knew her.

Chapter 30
DENIAL

The end of January and beginning of February brought Scott Peterson nothing but bad news. The police were focusing on him with increasing intensity. His in-laws were criticizing him in the media for selling Laci's Land Rover and picking a realtor to sell the couple's home. He had been recorded on a phone conversation talking with his parents about giving away McKenzie, the couple's golden retriever. And on February 9, the *National Enquirer* published nude photographs of Amber Frey taken years earlier when she considered becoming a model.

Scott wasn't looking anything like a devoted husband, never mind a man clinging to the hope that his missing wife might still be found alive.

The timing couldn't have been worse: Laci's due date was February 10.

Laci's family and her friends held a candlelight vigil at East La Loma Park at sunset.

Scott was absent.

Why, police might have wondered, wasn't Scott beside himself that day? Where was the tearful phone call to his mother or father? Why wasn't he surrounded by loved ones? Why wasn't he in church late into the night, praying for Laci's safe return?

Maybe he needed a girlfriend to show him what to do—someone he wanted to seduce, who also happened to be grieving. Then he could have just mimicked her.

The more isolated he was, the less human he looked.

He was a much better supporting actor than leading man.

And people were leaving Scott's side. He seemed resigned to it now. The tide had been going out a long time.

On a recorded phone call, Amber Frey told him she was signing off. "Okay. Um . . . I can't really say in light of current events," she started, "but, um, I don't know really the right . . . right words to say but I'm just going to say it. . . ."

"Okay," Scott said.

"However it comes out."

"Yeah?"

"I think right now for me, Scott, and really everything that has happened in the past fifty-plus days for myself and . . . and the family and you and everything that's going on right now . . . I think it would be best if you and I didn't talk anymore until there's resolution in this whole . . ."

"Yeah," Scott said. "I agree with that."

"Good," she said. "Good."

"You're right."

"Okay, well, that wasn't so hard."

"No, it's the right thing."

"Huh?" Amber asked.

"It's the right thing, so, yeah," Scott said.

"Okay. So is there anything you want to say before, um, I say good-bye?"

"Yes, I mean, you know, I see the reason. Oh, well, and just be well."

Oh, well? He used to be able to do better than that. The reflex machine was faltering. The mask was slipping away.

"Likewise," Amber said.

"Okay," Scott said. "I hope to talk to you in the future."

"Okay, Scott."

"Good-bye for now."

"Huh?" Amber asked.

"Good-bye for now."

"Good life now?"

"Good-bye for now," Scott repeated.

"Good-bye, Scott."

Scott Peterson was alone. And the bad news just kept coming.

Janet Ilse and Katy Hansen both disclosed that they had had romantic relationship with him. Police found their stories believable.

The portrait of Scott was getting more and more detailed.

In a meeting with Detective Buehler, one of Laci's friends named Renee Tomlinson reported a troubling conversation she had had with Scott and Laci's friend Heather Richardson. Heather had told Renee that Laci had gone for a high-tech, 3-D ultrasound procedure because Scott was extremely worried about the baby having any birth defect. The couple were prepared to abort Conner if problems were discovered. And it seemed to Heather that Scott was the one who had pushed both the ultrasound and the idea of terminating Laci's pregnancy in the case of any abnormal finding.

When Laci had first learned she was pregnant, Scott had told her sister-in-law, Rosemarie Rocha, "I was kind of hoping for infertility." Now it seemed he had been hoping for an abortion. And Sharon Rocha had wondered whether Laci's abdominal cramping during the weeks prior to her disappearance might have been due to Scott poisoning her to terminate her pregnancy.

It sounded like Scott had been campaigning to prevent Conner's birth from the day the boy was conceived. Because, for him, birth had always equaled death. There would be no joy for him bringing new life into the world because his own life had been a misery—slow strangulation—from day one.

By the end of January, the police made it known that Scott was the sole suspect in the disappearance of his wife and unborn child.

They pressed Scott to sit for an official polygraph. Instead, he made an aborted attempt to have Amber Frey secretly join him for one with an expert named Melvin King, a retired lieutenant for the Fresno Police Department. The polygraphs done by King could be kept completely confidential, with no record made of the results.

Scott was probably hoping his "mask of sanity" would foil the test. If not, he could deny ever having had it done.

Deny, deny, deny. Jackie had given him the game plan—her life plan—weeks before.

The polygraph never took place. According to King, Scott canceled his appointment, stating that his girlfriend had refused to come with him. And after Detective Brocchini contacted King and filled him in on the investigation, he told Scott he would be better off not rescheduling, and instead sitting for an official test given by the police.

On February 18, Modesto police searched Scott Peterson's house again. They noted the fact that baby Conner's nursery had been turned into a storage room. They found Scott's three fake diplomas in a closet. And they found his wedding ring in a duffel bag. McKenzie, Scott's golden retriever, was gone, staying with Scott's half brother Joe in San Diego.

Police also searched Scott's new Dodge truck, purchased with money from the sale of Laci's Land Rover, and his storage locker at Security Public Storage in Fresno.

In the truck, they found collection notices from the contractor who had installed the Petersons' pool, along with evidence Scott had resigned from the Del Rio Country Club and was trying to sell his membership.

In the storage locker, they found Laci and Scott's wedding album, in a metal wastepaper basket.

Fake diplomas in the closet. Conner's room emptied out. Scott's wedding band off his finger. His wedding album in the trash. McKenzie gone. Unpaid bills. A letter resigning from the country club.

Scott was like an actor walking offstage for the last time. He was shedding props left and right.

He told Anne Bird, his half sister, that he had decided to stop using his real name (just as his dad reportedly had so many years before) and call himself Cal. It kind of went with the rakish goatee he was growing.

A few nights later, according to Anne, Scott told her a disturbing story. The two of them were watching *Murder She Wrote* and eating BLT sandwiches (go figure). The main house in the television program reminded Scott of a bed-and-breakfast where Laci and he had spent the night in Mendocino, California.

From Anne's book, *Witness: 33 Reasons My Brother Scott Peterson Is Guilty:* "One day Laci and I went for a walk," Scott said, "and we ended up in a part of town we'd never seen before. We came across a small cemetery, with an even smaller cemetery just beyond it. The small cemetery was all overgrown with weeds, and the headstones were really small, so we assumed it was a pet cemetery."

But it wasn't a pet cemetery.

Laci and Scott climbed the fence and looked at the headstones.

"They were really old," Scott told Anne, "and really overgrown, and it was hard to read them. But then we read one and realized that it wasn't a pet cemetery at all. It was a children's cemetery. It was full of little children."

Scott stared directly at Anne. He looked as though he might start to cry.

"Laci started crying. She was very upset. She wanted to fix up the place. She wanted to clear out the brush and plant beautiful flowers and make it nice for the children. It was just, you know, it was just really sad."

Anne was transfixed. She felt Scott was trying to tell her something. "What happened?" she asked.

"Nothing," Scott said. "We left the cemetery and went back to town."

Perhaps a children's cemetery was the best symbol of Scott Peterson's tragic existence. He hadn't made it out of his own childhood alive, after all. Maybe standing there in front of the headstones of other dead children in Mendocino that day, he was taken aback by the way his throat was tightening, that he was finding it hard to swallow. Maybe he was close to tears himself and had no idea why. And that could have been a start. Because confusion always precedes enlightenment.

Maybe he squinted at something in the distance, cocked his head at a whisper of truth he was struggling to hear, a whisper from the timid, tortured little boy inside him.

Maybe if he and Laci had sat down in the overgrown grass and just let themselves talk—about whether the children buried around them had had any idea that they were dying, about what their fears might have been once they knew, about what losing them had done to their parents, about whether they were well loved, about who they might have grown up to be if they hadn't been buried at one or two or three years old, then maybe some sort of miracle could have happened. Maybe an almost imperceptible hairline crack could have formed in the mask of Scott Peterson. A beginning of empathy, of rebirth.

People have the power to heal one another.

I have seen it done, again and again, by true lovers.

But neither one of them could do it. Laci wanted to pretty the place up, make it "nice" for the buried children, as if that was any answer to the terrible suffering the headstones testified to. And Scott probably agreed, relieved that his sadness seemed suddenly to lift with the idea of buying some sunflowers to plant around the graves.

That was as deep as either of them was able to dig into each other's pain.

Deny. Deny. Deny.

Chapter 31
TRUTH

The Modesto police were anything but content to stay on the surface. They were digging deeper and deeper, hiring an expert on facial expressions to analyze Scott's television appearances, reviewing the conclusions of a voice analyst commissioned by a local television network, listening for any revelation in his taped phone calls. It was as if the work Scott Peterson had never done looking into his psyche, opening the abcess of his own destruction, probing his inability to resonate with the pain of others, looking behind his mask of sanity, was now being done by detectives.

On March 5, the Modesto Police Department officially declared the Laci Peterson case a homicide, reclassifying it from a missing person investigation.

They continued sifting through thousands of leads from the public, continued interviewing anyone they could find who had known Scott or Laci Peterson.

Then, just before 5:00 P.M. on April 13, police responded to a call from two residents of Cerrito, California, whose dog had found the badly decomposed body of a baby that had washed ashore from the San Francisco Bay. It was lying on its back, its head tilted upward.

The three-and-a-half-pound fetus was pronounced dead by the town's fire captain.

Its condition was grotesque, owing to exposure to the elements. Its skin was gray. Its genitals were gone. Nylon twine was tangled around its neck. Its right arm was nearly severed.

At autopsy, Dr. Brian Peterson (his last name a coincidence) of the Contra Costa Coroner's Facility would be unable to establish whether the fetus had ever taken a breath.

It was as if all the darkness from the past, all the destruction everyone had denied, had finally washed ashore, for everyone to see: Jackie's being placed in Nazareth House after the murder of her father John, the horrific abuse she had to have witnessed (or suffered) while there, her giving up two of her own babies, her reported desire to give up a third, Lee Peterson's growing up in poverty and trying to conceal it with Ferrari and Rolls-Royce automobiles, his reported discomfort living with his own children, the spiritual murder of a little boy named Scott Lee Peterson who had trouble breathing at birth and who was strangled psychologically at home.

Now the toll was undeniable. Now a dead baby had been found by the Bay.

Not a "shiny" baby. No "Golden Boy."

Birth equals death.

You can't outdistance the past.

The truth always wins.

*Lee*ta Helen Latham Hixon abandons Jackie Peterson, who marries *Lee* Peterson after abandoning two children born out of wedlock, and then begets Scott *Lee* Peterson, who is suffocated to death psychologically in childhood, and then drowns his own unborn son.

A day after the discovery of the dead fetus, a woman's body washed ashore east of Brooks Island, where Scott had said he had gone fishing the day Laci went missing.

The body was missing its head and both legs below the knee. The rib cage and spine were exposed. Every internal organ was missing from the abdominal cavity (consistent with being consumed by fish), except for the uterus, which was torn open. The body was clad in a bra and shredded remnants of maternity pants.

At autopsy, Dr. Peterson found fractures to the woman's fifth, sixth, and ninth ribs, consistent with a violent blow prior to death.

As Catherine Crier notes in her book *A Deadly Game*, the condition of mother and child were most consistent with Conner having exited Laci's body through a rupture in her abdomen caused by pressure build-up from bacteria and gases, a horrific process known as coffin birth.

There could be no more stark or tragic symbol of having been fathered by a dead man.

Chapter 32
THE ARREST

Scott's days as a free man were rapidly drawing to a close.

Since he had stopped driving his own truck, police had to use the wiretap on his phone to locate him. On April 16, they pinpointed his location as 3949 Le Cresta Avenue in San Diego, Anne Bird's adoptive parents' home, where he had been staying while they were away.

Agents were dispatched to keep tabs on him. When they first spotted him, they were surprised to see that he had dyed his new goatee, his hair, and his eyebrows blond with a reddish orange tint.

He looked quite different. But, then, again, he had always been wearing a disguise of one kind or another. It was second nature to him.

Police obtained an arrest warrant for Peterson and, on April 18, began following him in his dark red 1984 Mercedes Benz, which he had purchased under the name Jacqueline Peterson.

Scott knew he was being followed. He drove onto the freeway, then off, then back on again. He stopped in the breakdown lane, then pulled back into traffic. He exited and drove around Rancho Santa Fe, near his parents' home, stopping and starting, making U-turns, then speeding away.

While he was leading agents on this wild ride, Scott phoned his half brother Joe. He told him he couldn't meet him to play golf. He was being followed by investigators.

He didn't sound any more concerned than if he had been calling to cancel on account of rain.

"Where are you?" Joe asked. "Are you—well, I don't want to ask you that, I guess."

"I'm on Genessee," Scott said. "These guys, they know I'm onto them . . . I think I'd better skip it [golf] because I don't think I want a picture of me in the press playing. . . ."

"I saw the picture where everybody is leaving flowers and stuffed animals and everything in front of your house," Joe said.

"Oh, yeah?"

"Yeah. Any indication when they may identify these bodies?"

"No."

Scott maintained that police would learn the bodies were not those of Laci and Conner.

"Yeah, that's what I think . . . ," Joe agreed.

"Have fun [golfing], guys," Scott said.

"Sorry, bro."

"It's not your fault," Scott replied. "Thanks for the thought, though."

Police had hoped to wait to arrest Scott until DNA tests confirmed the identities of the bodies to be those of Laci and Conner, but radio newscasters began reporting that the results were, indeed, due at any moment. The police began to worry Scott might hear the news and try to flee the area. They pulled him over.

Scott didn't resist being placed in handcuffs.

According to Catherine Crier's research into police records, when Scott was asked why he thought he was being arrested, he guessed it might be his erratic driving.

An officer suggested he take another guess.

"Well," Scott said, "Modesto wants me about a murder."

He asked the officers which agency they worked for. Then he asked, "Have they found my wife and son?"

Scott was transported to the station in an unmarked police car. At 11:35 A.M. he was placed under arrest for murder.

A search of Scott's car would reveal nearly $15,000 in cash, a filet knife, a double-edged dagger with a T handle, a folding saw, a shovel, duct tape, binoculars, a mask and snorkel, a Leatherman tool, a fishing rod and reel, a dozen pairs of shoes, including waterproof boots and hiking boots, and several pairs of pants, several shirts, jackets, underwear, socks, neckties, and sweaters. He also had four cell phones, a credit card in Jackie Peterson's name, another credit card issued to Anne Bird, his brother John's driver's license, some Mexican currency, sleeping pills, and a dozen tablets of Viagra. And he had one more thing: a map to American Bodyworks, where Amber Frey worked, which he had downloaded from Mapquest that very day.

Scott Peterson seemed to have been on the verge of leaving the country, apparently for Mexico, leaving behind a life that he had never truly lived, a life that had been an act, until the script took a turn in a direction he could not abide. Then the murdered boy inside him, filled with helplessness, grief, and rage, believing that his rebirth would require the deaths of others, came center stage.

Scott was leaving with cash and Viagra, two tools he needed to achieve the only freedom he had ever known, the anonymity and rush of romancing women while remaining unknown to them. It had been the only way he could get close—at least physically—to anyone.

Until Amber.

Why did Scott have directions to Amber's office?

I believe he wanted to see her one more time. Because I believe he knew her as someone truly and intensely alive—and because she had helped him sense something alive inside himself. What started as a seduction, pure and simple, another one-act play that Scott figured he could fit in on the side, had become something very close to love, maybe love itself, and it had partly fueled the perfect storm in his psyche.

He had never felt anything like love before, after all. He had observed his mother and father intently, mimicked them, and said he loved them, when he actually feared and loathed them. He had romanced many other women, but always as another man, never himself. He had married a woman whose focus on perfection promised him that she would never see the darkness in his soul, nor bring him face-to-face with it.

Maybe he even wanted to tell Amber the truth about what he had done, to be known wholly for once, to take the mask of sanity completely off his panicked, distorted, unborn face for more than a split second, to *feel* what it was like to be *seen*, to take the first few real breaths in his "life."

Of course things could have gone horribly wrong. He could have asked Amber to tell him she loved him in return, or asked her to come with him, and become enraged when she backed away in fear. He could have seen her as the embodiment of everyone else who had failed to see him as human, failed to embrace him as flawed, beginning with his mother, Jackie, and father, Lee. And he could have killed her, and then himself.

He could have left Ayiana, Amber's precious twenty-month-old daughter, without a mother, just as Jackie was left without her mother when she was sent to Nazareth House, just as Anne

Bird and her half brother, Don Chapman, were left without a mother when Jackie put them up for adoption, just as he himself was left without a mother during the days he lived in a cold plastic chamber as an infant, unable to breathe, and during the thirty years he lived without a mother who truly loved him.

Chapter 33
COOKIES

Scott was read his constitutional rights and photographed. He was then allowed three calls.

First he called Kirk McAllister, his attorney. Next he called his mother, Jackie. Then he called Heather and Mike Richardson to tell them he wouldn't be able to send them the special lavender-petal cookies he had planned to.

Organize murder defense. Say good-bye to Mom. Apologize for not sending cookies. It's hard to say which he would have picked if he had only been allowed one call.

He asked to make a fourth call, in fact. He wanted to leave a message at Tradecorp to tell his employer he wouldn't be in for a while.

The police told him that one could wait.

Scott had been arrested for murder, his mug shot had been taken, and he was still thinking about whether he'd get in trouble for missing work.

I don't think he was faking. The walls around his soul were that thick. He wasn't afraid or grief stricken or angry. He wasn't even there.

He was also worried he would be disappointing his niece that night. He had promised to take her to the movies.

He even apologized to the police for his erratic driving earlier in the day.

Scott was driven to the Stanislaus County jail and placed in leg irons and waist chains. His hands remained cuffed.

En route, Detectives Buehler and Grogan, who were transporting Scott, were informed that DNA testing had confirmed that the bodies that had washed up from the San Francisco Bay were those of Laci and Conner Peterson.

When Scott was told, he shed a single tear.

About an hour later, when Buehler and Grogan made a pit stop at the In & Out Burger in Bakersfield, California, Scott asked for a double-double cheesburger, fries, and a vanilla shake.

Scott's fast-food order while shackled made me think of a story Anne Bird had told me about a visit with her mother, Jackie, after Scott's arrest on murder charges.

"The last time I went to see Jackie," she said, "she said it was a perfect day, even though Scott was in jail, and Laci and Conner were gone. I stopped by her house, and we had cottage cheese and saltines and sat in the garden, and she kept smiling and smiling, saying, 'This is a perfect day.' And she showed me a note on the plate of saltines from Lee that said, 'Have a nice day.'"

I myself remember dialing Jackie's cell phone while researching this book, after Scott had been found guilty, sentenced to death, and confined to a prison cell at San Quentin. I got her greeting. It was Lee, sounding as if he didn't have a care in the world. "Hi, my bride can't pick up right now," he half sang. "But leave a message. She'll get back to you*uuuu*. 'Bye-'bye."

Chapter 34
"THIS IS THE BEST PLACE FOR ME"

While incarcerated, Scott Peterson sent a number of e-mails to his parents. He addressed them to "Dad Jackie." I obtained copies.

In the first e-mail, from July 14, 2003, Scott told his parents that while his "emotional tide changes" could fill many pages, that while he would feel "great joy" were he to share his memories of Laci with them, he was loath to do so given that his e-mails were being monitored by authorities.

The *tides,* of course, hadn't exactly been kind to Scott. They had swept the bodies of his victims out of the San Francisco Bay onto shore. No wonder he didn't want to dwell on that.

Scott wrote instead about how fortunate he felt to have many photographs of Laci with him in his cell. Some of the best ones had come along with hate mail, but that didn't bother him at all. He'd just rip off the obscenities and death threats and keep the images.

He also had a number of shots of other family members. He wrote that he managed to find some humor in pictures of his nephew Tommy, usually with food "covering his face." And he connected images of Tommy with his unborn son: "I can imagine that Conner would resemble him in many ways . . ." For this reason, Scott told his parents, he especially treasured a photograph of Tommy in his arms at Tommy's christening.

He then moved on to talking about the inmates in the cells adjacent to his own and about books he has been reading—all of them, including *Alaska, Undaunted Courage, Nothing Else Like It on Earth,* and *Travels with Charley,* about outdoor adventure and "people moving into things they do not know."

"My sleep continues to be interrupted," he wrote, "by nightmares and emotional state, but aided by my move in cells [this one being quieter]. The new cell is darker and further from the drunk tanks. As long as I wait for justice I believe this to be the best place for me."

In a sign that he had no idea who had been bleeding him emotionally for thirty years, he told his parents, "Exercise, reading and visits from Matt [an attorney] are helpful. The true lifeline is the telephone and your visits."

In a second e-mail, a long one dated September 21, 2003, Scott sent his parents a "humorous story concerning McKenzie," the golden retriever Laci had given him, that had occurred while he and Laci were living on a ranch in San Luis Obispo.

McKenzie had the habit of going to the end of the lane that led to the ranch, sitting on the shoulder of the highway, and jumping into the cars that stopped to make sure he was safe.

Scott had, therefore, built a fence around his ranch house.

There were many other dogs in the neighborhood, including three new litters of puppies born to an Australian shepherd and a Queensland that lived at a neighbor's house.

"In that hovel," Scott wrote, there were about twenty puppies, each one about a foot tall, "with little razor-sharp teeth. Piles of blue and red fur could be seen and heard boiling in fights at the front house at all hours. Villainous creatures engaged in pack-scraps for dominance."

Villainous puppies? Scott was coming close to his core truth. Birth equals death. Babies are evil, worthy of abandonment.

"Laci and I were in the workshop," he went on, "when we heard a frantic high pitched chorus of yapping, snarling and growling moving toward us."

It was the puppies. They were chasing McKenzie, who was utterly terrified. "The hair on the back of his neck was up, a Mohawk of fear, his eyes were pleading to be saved, his lower jaw was trembling and clenched. He was trying to escape from an angry beehive of maniacal puppies that were pursuing him from the projects."

Puppies intent on destroying everything around them. Puppies from the "projects," attempting to drag McKenzie into poverty—or worse.

Scott wrote that he and Laci had to save McKenzie from thousands of "puppy teeth."

Despite kneeling down and trying to stop the puppies like goalies stopping pucks, Scott and Laci could not hold all of them back. They pursued McKenzie into the Petersons' front yard, up past the barn, then circled back, relentless, a "pack of little Satans."

"McKenzie crashed down the hill," Scott wrote, desperate to escape "the needle fangs" of the puppies. He crossed a creek, raced back, and barely made it into the bed of Scott's truck.

"He was on his feet as he peered over the side of the truck down upon his mean spirited mob of pursuers. They yapped and gave off upper register growls, McKenzie panted, and you could see a smile in his eyes."

Then, he wrote:

THE END

Killer puppies. Jackie and Lee must have loved it.

Scott had shown all his cards. All through Laci's pregnancy, he had felt as though Conner was pursuing him, that he would rip him to shreds once he was born, destroy him.

But Scott had won. He had turned birth into death, drowning his wife in a pool (the creek in his e-mail), then putting her body in the bed of his truck and dumping her in the Bay.

And as his homemade concrete anchors had dragged her body underwater, he had seen his own reflection, his own smiling eyes.

Chapter 35
TRIAL

Scott's family retained famed criminal defense attorney Mark Geragos to represent him. High-profile clients were nothing new to Geragos; he had also represented Congressman Gary Condit, whose intern Chandra Levy disappeared and was found murdered. And he represented Michael Jackson for a period of time when the entertainer was accused of child sexual assault.

Geragos did not, apparently, have Scott evaluated by a psychiatrist, nor is there any indication that he or Scott himself ever considered a plea of not guilty by reason of insanity. Scott's contention was that he had not murdered his wife and unborn child, *period*, not that he had done so while mentally ill.

But, in my opinion as a forensic psychiatrist, an insanity plea would have spoken to the truth.

Scott Peterson was indeed insane, suffering with two severe and related psychiatric conditions when he took Laci and Conner's lives.

One of those conditions is best described as a dissociative disorder, the hallmark of which is a disruption in a person's sense of identity. In some cases the disruption is so severe that the individual has multiple personalities, but it can also cause a person to feel or act "unreal," removed from reality, like an automaton.

Whether or not Scott Peterson knew it himself, the prolonged period of time in childhood during which he was dehumanized—psychologically strangled—had resulted in his breaking free of his core feelings and adopting a machinelike identity to navigate the world.

Having done so, the *real* Scott, the tortured boy who had grown into a man, was not really in control at all. His "life" was essentially a series of stereotyped behavior patterns that he used to obtain sex.

Without the ability to feel, he could not empathize with the suffering of others. He could not consider others fully human, for he did not feel human himself. He was, therefore, able to lie without remorse, and to kill without conscience.

He was not only insane, he was not really a person.

Understood this way, Scott's call to the Richardsons apologizing for not getting them their cookies makes sense. He owed them cookies. He needed to call them to tell them that he couldn't send them. Because those were the facts. It didn't matter how he was *feeling* at the moment, having just been arrested for murder. Because he was *dissociated* from his feelings, floating free from his core, a person imitating a person.

Just think of Scott apologizing to police for driving erratically before being pulled over and handcuffed. To the internal operator of Scott's mask—that fractured being trying to fool everyone into thinking he was a normal person—saying he was sorry must have seemed like the thing to do to pass for a real person. Maybe he'd heard the rule from his mother: if you put people out and waste their time, you apologize. Or else.

But the words didn't strike police officers as heartfelt or appropriate under the circumstances. And that was because the words were not connected to any real feelings. They were not spoken by a real person.

Think of Scott lying in bed, unmoved, after Janet Ilse burst in on him and Laci. No guilt, no fear, no embarrassment. Not human. Dissociated from genuine feelings.

Dissociative disorder.

The second condition Scott suffers from is, indeed, antisocial personality disorder. A textbook case. His symptoms include deceitfulness, impulsivity, irresponsibility, and lack of remorse. That condition, too, would render him unable to exercise genuine free will.

How could Scott use the concepts of right and wrong to choose how to behave, after all, if right and wrong meant nothing to him *emotionally*? If he was not moved in any way by morality, if he never felt shame or even anxiety when trampling on the rights or feelings of another person, then what was to stop him from doing so?

Healthy people refrain from hurting one another largely because they know what it is to be hurt. They *empathize* with one another.

Scott's ability to do that had been shattered in childhood.

None of these issues would be raised during his trial. In fact, Mark Geragos would call witness after witness to testify to how normal Scott was, what a polite and reliable person he was, how he couldn't possibly be a heartless killer.

Nothing could be further from the truth.

And the jury would know it in their hearts.

Jury selection began in early March. The trial started on June 1 in the Redwood City Courthouse. It would last five months.

A parade of witnesses were called, but Amber Frey was clearly the star. Her testimony that Scott had continued to lie to her and pursue her romantically, pretending that he was traveling in Europe with buddies after Laci went missing, was impossible to reconcile with the public face Scott had shown—that of a husband grieving the loss of his wife and refusing to give up hope that she would be found alive.

That disconnect, together with Scott placing himself at the very location where Laci and Conner's bodies were recovered, would probably have been enough to seal his fate.

But there was also the fact that Scott had fashioned homemade anchors from cement, that he had used the stock phrase "Laci is missing" when he first called his mother-in-law to tell her that Laci wasn't at home that fateful Christmas Eve day, that he had sold Laci's Land Rover and tried to sell their home.

Laci is missing. Sounds like a robot, doesn't it? Insane.

The defense had to make it sound normal.

He sold his missing wife's car and tried to sell the house she loved. Sounds perfectly heartless, inhuman. Insane.

The defense had to make it sound perfectly normal.

They couldn't even come close.

Despite the dramatic play-by-play offered by networks and newspapers and magazines, the case was always what California Attorney General Bill Lockyer had called a slam dunk.

On November 12, the jury returned its verdict. They found Scott guilty of the first-degree murder of his wife, Laci, and the second-degree murder of his unborn son, Conner.

Scott did not shed a tear. Neither did his mother. His father wasn't even in court that day.

Chapter 36
DEATH

In the state of California, a first-degree murder conviction is punishable either by life in prison without the possibility of parole or by death.

On November 30, 2004, the penalty phase of Scott Peterson's double murder trial began.

Jurors heard first from Brent Rocha, Laci's thirty-one-year-old brother. Choking back tears, he said, "I don't think I've ever heard her more excited than the day she called me up to tell me she was pregnant. She was going to be a great mother."

He spoke of being haunted by the tragedy, waking in the middle of the night with images of his sister's death, constantly being distracted during the day by the thought that he had lost her forever. "I try to remember the good memories we have with each other," he said, "but they are overshadowed all the time by what happened to her, how she died, by maybe her knowing who did it."

Laci's half sister, Amy, told the jury that holidays would never be the same without her. "She brought everyone together," Amy said. "She was kind of the life of the holidays." But it was much more than that. "I still can't imagine my life going on without her," she said.

Laci's stepfather, Ron Grantski, also had to fight back tears. "I wish I could be the one gone and not her," he told jurors. "Part of my heart is gone."

But it was Sharon Rocha whose grief transcended even the drama of the moment, speaking to the pain of every mother who has ever lost a child.

Prosecutor David Harris asked Sharon how Mother's Day had been for her.

"I laid on the floor and I cried most of the day because [Laci] should have been there and she should have been a mother also, and that was taken away from her," she said. She then turned to Scott and yelled, "She wanted to be a mother!"

Scott did not react.

Imagine if you were an innocent, normal man in the situation in which he found himself. You would be on your feet, screaming, crying, "I didn't do it, Mom. You have to believe me! I loved her. I would never hurt her. I'd give my life for her."

But Scott Peterson wasn't even in that courtroom. Not really. He had all but taken his leave of this world before he ever met Laci, before he ever fathered Conner.

"She would call me every time she went to the doctor and let me know the results," Sharon went on. "She gave me a copy of the sonogram. It's the only picture I have of the baby, and he was a baby. You could see his little body."

Sharon spoke of saying good-bye to her daughter before her funeral. She wept as she testified. "I knew that I needed to spend some time with her and to have the opportunity to say good-bye to her alone and I knew she was in the casket and I knew the baby was there and I knew she didn't have arms to hold him either. . . ."

"Every morning when I get up I cry," she said later. "It takes me a long time just to be able to get out of the house. I keep thinking, 'Why did this happen?' I miss her. I wanted to know my grandson. I wanted Laci to be a mother. I wanted to hear her be called 'Mom.'"

The courtroom was silent. Many of the spectators were in tears. Because a woman who had lost a daughter she truly loved had shared her very real and excruciating pain. And people lucky enough to have had childhoods not marred by severe psychological violence retain the inexplicable, magnificent, immeasurable, God-given ability to resonate with the suffering of others. They have empathy.

Everyone is born with it. It is what connects us as human beings, one to another. And it is fragile.

Children are less resilient than people think. They can have their empathy extinguished by abuse or neglect or the kind of quiet, relentless emotional suffocation that took Scott Peterson's life from him.

Lee and Jackie Peterson themselves spoke on behalf of their son before the jury that November day.

Jackie testified that her father had been murdered when she was two and that she had been placed in an orphanage. She said her life changed forever when she met Lee.

"He gave me the family I always wanted," she said. "We called ourselves 'the Brady Bunch,' there were so many of us."

She asserted that her son was nurturing and kind and had

been harassed by the police and stalked by the media and wrongly portrayed as a devil. She described him as a victim.

Lee Peterson said he had "great respect" for his son and loved him very much.

He told of Scott's work ethic, that while he was growing up he "always had at least two and sometimes three jobs."

Scott's half sister Susan Caudillo also lined up behind Scott. "We've gone through so much as a family," she said, "but we're sticking by [Scott] one hundred percent. But I don't think my parents will make it if he goes."

And Scott's brother John, asked by Mark Geragos whether Scott should be sentenced to death, responded, "I can't even imagine; I'd be wrecked. He's my little brother. I love him."

The problem was, of course, that the Petersons could not tell the real story of Scott Peterson. They could not sway jurors because they were still portraying him as a normal man who had grown up in a normal family.

Nothing could be further from the truth. And only the truth can move people.

Scott Peterson was the victim of a perfect psychological storm that began with the murder of his grandfather on December 20, 1945, a tragedy that precipitated a tidal wave of losses that thundered through three generations and, ultimately, drowned Laci and Conner. The storm had destroyed Scott's capacity to empathize with others, harvested his free will, removed from his soul the inborn, internal restraint that keeps human beings from destroying one another, stolen from him any joy he might see in new life coming into the world, made him see birth as the equivalent of death.

What Scott's family needed to testify to wasn't how kind and helpful and industrious he was. They needed to testify to how ill and inhuman he was, how he had been born an innocent child and turned, through no fault of his own, into a cold-blooded killer, how he was already dead and gone himself, how executing him would only be a reflection of the same inhumanity that had infected him.

They needed to call for mercy for a man incapable of it.

But none of that would make very good conversation over tea in the garden. You'd never hear Jan Brady saying such things about Greg.

The jury deliberated eight hours and twenty-three minutes, then returned a unanimous verdict of death.

Scott Peterson sat stoically as the decision was read.

Jackie and Lee Peterson shed not a tear.

Spectators outside the courtroom cheered as the verdict was announced, none of them noticing that whatever had infected Scott Peterson, destroying his empathy, had become contagious— to them.

Afterword

Having interviewed, treated, and testified about dozens of murderers, rapists, and other violent men and women, I have come to know that no one is born evil. People are born good, and then life circumstances conspire to destroy their inborn capacity for empathy—their humanity.

Like Scott Peterson's, the stories of destruction can reach back decades and generations, the early chapters hidden until we resolve to resurrect them, to understand them.

And no one, not even those we call monsters, is beyond that understanding.

Scott Peterson sits on death row. Laci Peterson and Conner Peterson lie buried in a cemetery. But neither the transcript of Scott's trial nor the headstones of his victims tell the story of the perfect psychological storm that claimed all their lives.

We are tempted, always, to blame someone exclusively for such a tragedy, to point to Scott Peterson as evil incarnate, or to point to his parents, Jackie and Lee, and hold them responsible for creating him, or to point to Leeta Helen Hixon Latham, Jackie's mother, and hold her responsible for giving up her children and placing them in harm's way, or to point to Robert Sewell, the odd-jobs worker who killed Jackie's father, or to point to Sewell's parents for raising a man who would kill for several hundred dollars.

Yet we know that nearly unbearable grief compromised Jackie's ability to mother. And if we knew Leeta Latham's life story, we would understand why she could not bear to raise her children alone. And if we knew Robert Sewell's story we would understand why he placed almost no value on human life.

The more you look for the truth, the further back you search for it, the more you realize that there is no original evil left in the world. Everyone is just recycling pain.

This work I do, then, is oddly reassuring to me. For there are no monsters that spring, fully grown, onto the planet. There are only vulnerable children, destroyed by those who have been destroyed themselves, made hungry for the blood of others.

Can they be saved? Can they be resurrected, healed?

Can the cycle be broken?

I believe it is possible, but not always, and not with any predictability. I know it requires more empathy from us, not less. I know it requires some raw material to work with—a person in whom the light of life still burns, however dimly. And I know it requires a certain amount of luck—the right moments between the right human beings, whether teacher and student, therapist and patient, husband and wife, or between lovers.

The words of the great poet Rainer Maria Rilke come to mind. I leave you with them:

> Perhaps all the dragons of our lives
> are princesses who are only waiting to
> see us once, beautiful and brave.
> Perhaps everything terrible is in
> its deepest being something
> that needs our love.